THE CREATIVE

Vegetarian

COOKBOOK

COURAGE
BOOKS
AN IMPRINT OF RUNNING PRESS
PHILADELPHIA • LONDON

Watercolor illustrations by Sally Brewer
Designed by Stonecastle Graphics
Edited by Jillian Stewart and Kate Cranshaw
American adaptation: Josephine Bacon

4949
© 1997 CLB International, Godalming, Surrey, U.K.
This edition first published in the United States by
Courage Books, an imprint of Running Press Book Publishers

Printed in Singapore
9   8   7   6   5   4   3   2   1
Digit on the right indicates the number of this printing
Library of Congress Cataloging-in-Publication Number 96-71945
ISBN 0-7624-0098-6

This book was produced by CLB International
Godalming, Surrey, U.K.

Published by Courage Books, an imprint of
Running Press Book Publishers
125 South Twenty-second Street
Philadelphia, Pennsylvania 19103-4399

Contents

Introduction

Choosing to avoid eating meat is no longer a cranky thing to do. Every year thousands of people decide to cut out the meat, fish, and poultry from their diet and turn vegetarian. No longer are vegetarians made to feel like freaks. Their needs are becoming increasingly well catered for by food manufacturers, and even restaurants are now offering imaginative vegetarian dishes on their menus. But what do you prepare for everyday meals or for those special occasions when guests are expected? Putting into practice the decision to become a vegetarian can be daunting – as can the announcement by a member in a family of confirmed carnivores to turn vegetarian.

First must come a basic understanding of what constitutes a healthy vegetarian diet. Cutting out meat products that are high in fat is a positively healthy step to take, but be careful that you don't just substitute equally high-fat cheese and eggs in their place. Make the effort to introduce a wide range of plant foods, and remember the advice to include four or five portions of fresh fruit (or fruit juice) and vegetables in your diet each day.

While fruit and vegetables are nutritious foods, they do not contain significant amounts of protein. That is left to the plant protein foods. Cereal grains and their products such as wheat, oats, barley, rye (and flour, oatmeal, pasta and bulgar and couscous) rice, buckwheat, corn, sorghum, millet, triticale, quinoa, beans, dried peas, lentils, nuts, and seeds, as well as soya products such as tofu, are all suitable foods for building the protein content of the diet. Do remember, however, that plant protein foods such as these contain a lower quality protein than animal foods. This deficiency can easily be overcome by serving different types of protein together – a grain and a bean product, a nut and bean or grain – or by mixing a plant protein with a dairy product which will contain a higher quality protein in itself. This is never as complex as it seems – consider a cheese sandwich, baked beans on toast, or lasagne; all mix different forms of vegetarian proteins to give a perfect balance.

Research monitoring the health of vegetarians suggests that their diet is typically lower in fat than that of the average person, and that this has a beneficial effect on health. Cutting out meat and meat products, in particular, is an obvious way of reducing fat intake, particularly the intake of the less desirable saturated fat. A vegetarian diet that depends too much on dairy foods, however, would not necessarily be any lower in saturated fat, so try to include more of the lower-fat plant proteins.

A third aspect of balancing the diet is the fiber content. Ensuring there is sufficient fiber is important in maintaining a healthy digestive system. Whereas animal foods are devoid of fiber, all plant foods contain some fiber. Pulses or legumes (beans, peas, and lentils) whole-wheat and oats are especially fiber-rich. After the fiber, fat, and protein elements of the diet come the vitamins and minerals. Vitamins are vital for proper body functioning, with each vitamin performing a specific task. Vitamin C is only found in fresh fruits and vegetables, so ensuring a good daily intake of these foods is the basis of a good vitamin C supply. The B group of vitamins is found in cereals and nuts and in small amounts in a wide range of dairy and plant foods, with the exception of vitamin B12.

Vitamin B12 is found only in animal products – although small amounts have been traced in fermented soya products such as miso and in some seaweeds. Generally, though, it is assumed that vegetarians eating dairy foods will rely on cheese, eggs, and milk for their supply of vitamin B12, whereas vegans and others restricting dairy foods will need to include a fortified food, such as soya-based foods and foods made specifically for vegans, which are likely to have this crucial vitamin added. It is important to check the labels, for instance on fortified breakfast cereals.

The other vitamin that might pose a problem for vegetarians is vitamin D. We traditionally derive a large amount of vitamin D from fish and fish liver oils, but this vitamin is also found in certain dairy foods and is added to margarine and some milk products. Unlike other vitamins, we are also able to manufacture our own supply by the action of the sun on the skin. Ensuring regular outdoor exercise and fresh air will boost vitamin D levels, but the housebound and young people may be in extra need of this vitamin.

Finally, on the nutritional side there are minerals which, like vitamins, are required only in small amounts but which play a crucial role in health maintenance. The most significant mineral for vegetarians is iron, which is found in the richest concentrations in red meat and variety meats. Women of childbearing age and teenage girls are at greatest risk from anemia caused by a shortage of iron in the diet, so those following a vegetarian diet are at even greater risk. To ensure your diet is not mineral-deficient, eat plenty of green leaf vegetables, such as spinach, collard greens, and watercress, whole grains, wheatgerm, eggs, nuts, and dried apricots.

Following these simple nutritional steps will help to build the basis of a healthy vegetarian diet – now for the cooking!

Soups

Gone are the days when a soup without meat meant mixed vegetable! Today, just about any vegetable can take center stage in an exciting soup recipe all its own.

Soups make good use of all manner of fresh produce, combining everyday or more exotic vegetables with herbs and spices or basic storecupboard standbys into a wealth of differently styled dishes.

Soup can take the form of a light appetizer, a perfect prelude to a formal dinner, or at the other end of the scale, served with a hunk of bread, it can make a hearty, filling meal in itself. In between lies a range of soups that are ideal for a light midday or evening snack. Most soups can be conveniently prepared in advance and simply reheated when required.

Traditionally, soup has been regarded as a seasonal dish reserved for cold winter days. But just as salad can be enjoyed throughout the year, so soups have become standard fare for all seasons.

Turning the traditional on its head are light, chilled soups, perfect for summer days or evenings. The classic Vichysoisse (p.12), a creamy blend of leek and potato, is one such dish that tastes good hot, but purists would argue that it should always be served cold.

Recipes designed to be served chilled should be just that – not lukewarm, but allowed to cool thoroughly and then seasoned to taste before serving. The flavor of a good soup comes from careful seasoning, appropriate use of herbs and spices, but more importantly from a good basic broth. Rarely do soup recipes call simply for water; nearly all require broth to give a really good flavor base. Making vegetable broth at home is much easier and less time-consuming than the laborious meat-based broths. To make $2^1/2$ pints broth, sauté a chopped onion in a little oil, stir in a chopped carrot, a small, chopped turnip, and four chopped celery sticks with a few cabbage leaves or celery tops. Pour over $3^3/4$ pints cold water, bring to a boil, then simmer gently for $1-1^1/2$ hours, before straining. This broth will keep for up to 48 hours in the refrigerator.

If time is tight, use a commercial stock cube or concentrate instead. There are several good vegetarian stock products on the market, so you can experiment.

Home-made broth and most soups freeze well, but remember not to freeze recipes made with egg, cream, or yogurt as they might separate out and spoil the texture. When it comes to serving soup, don't forget to garnish carefully and to serve with bread, the fresher the better, the time-honored and still perfect accompaniment.

Cream of Cucumber —with Mint—

This delicious summer soup can be eaten hot, or chilled and served on ice for a refreshing change.

SERVES 4

3 large cucumbers
1 quart vegetable broth
Salt and freshly ground black pepper
2-3 sprigs fresh mint
1¼ cups light cream
4 Tbsps natural yogurt, to garnish

Cut one of the cucumbers in half and chop one half into small dice. Set the small dice to one side. Peel the remaining half and the other 2 cucumbers and roughly chop them into small pieces. Put the peeled cucumber, broth, and seasoning into a large saucepan. Remove the mint leaves from the sprig and add the stalks only to the pan. Bring gently to a boil, reduce the heat, and simmer gently for 25 minutes, or until cucumber is tender.

Remove the mint stalks from the soup and, using a blender or food processor, purée the soup until smooth. Return to the rinsed-out pan and stir in the light cream and the reserved, diced cucumber. Reheat gently for about 5 minutes. To serve, finely chop the mint leaves and add to the soup. Stir a tablespoon of yogurt into each bowl before serving.

Time: Preparation takes about 15 minutes, cooking takes about about 30 minutes.

Variation: Use a mixture of half broth and half light beer for an interesting variation.

Vichyssoise

This classic French soup is both simple and economical to make.

SERVES 4

3 large leeks
3 Tbsps butter or margarine
2-3 medium potatoes, peeled and sliced
3¾ pints vegetable broth
⅔ cup milk
Salt and freshly ground black pepper
3 Tbsps sour cream
Snipped chives, to garnish

Wash and trim the leeks, discarding the green parts. Slice the white part of the leeks thinly. Melt the butter or margarine in a large saucepan and sauté the leeks and potatoes for 10 minutes, stirring frequently until just softened. Add the broth and bring gently to a boil. Reduce the heat and simmer for 30 minutes. Allow to cool slightly, pour the soup into a blender or food processor, and blend until smooth.

Return soup to the rinsed-out pan. Stir in the milk, season, and bring gently to simmering point. Chill before serving. Garnish with sour cream and snipped chives.

Time: Preparation takes about 15 minutes, cooking takes about 45 minutes.

Serving Idea: Vichyssoise is traditionally served chilled, but serve this soup hot for a delicious change.

Sweet Potato Soup

Warm up your winter nights with this filling soup.

SERVES 4-6

4 Tbsps butter or margarine
1 large onion, minced
1 pound sweet potatoes, peeled and diced
1 cup carrots, peeled and diced
1 Tbsp chopped coriander (cilantro)
Grated rind and juice of 1 lemon
3 ¾ cups vegetable broth
Freshly ground black pepper

Melt the butter or margarine and cook the onion until transparent. Add the sweet potato and carrots and cook gently over a very low heat for 10-15 minutes, stirring occasionally. Add the coriander (cilantro), lemon rind, juice of half the lemon, broth, and pepper. Cover and simmer for 30-40 minutes. Blend until almost smooth, leaving some texture to the soup. Return to the pan and reheat until piping hot. Garnish with coriander (cilantro) leaves and serve immediately.

Time: Preparation takes 15 minutes, cooking takes 40-55 minutes.

Serving Idea: Serve with mixed grain rolls.

Cook's Tip: Fresh coriander (cilantro) should be stored in a pitcher of water in a cool place.

Easy Lentil Soup

A good old-fashioned soup which is sure to please all the family.

SERVES 4-6

1 cup split red lentils
2 Tbsps butter or margarine
1 medium onion, minced
2 stalks celery, finely diced
2 carrots, scrubbed and finely diced
Grated rind of 1 lemon
5 cups light vegetable broth
Salt and freshly ground black pepper

Pick over the lentils and remove any stones. Rinse well. Heat the butter or margarine in a saucepan and sauté the onion for 2-3 minutes. Add the diced celery and carrots and let the vegetables cook on low heat for 5-10 minutes. Stir in the lentils. Add the lemon rind, broth, and salt and pepper to taste. Bring to a boil, reduce the heat, and simmer for 15-20 minutes, until the vegetables are tender.

Roughly blend the soup in a blender, it should not be too smooth. Adjust the seasoning and reheat gently.

Time: Preparation takes about 10 minutes, cooking takes 15-20 minutes.

Serving Idea: Sprinkle with cheese and serve with hot toast.

Freezing: Freeze for up to 3 months.

Vegetable Soup

This hearty vegetable soup makes the most of traditional and unusual vegetables.

SERVES 4

2 Tbsps vegetable oil
1 large carrot, peeled and diced
1 large turnip, peeled and diced
2 leeks, washed and thinly sliced
2 potatoes, scrubbed and diced
2¹/₂ cups vegetable broth
1-pound can plum tomatoes, chopped
1 bay leaf
¹/₄ tsp dried savory or marjoram
¹/₂ cup soup pasta
Salt and freshly ground black pepper
¹/₂ cup fresh or frozen sliced green beans
¹/₂ cup okra, trimmed and sliced
¹/₂ cup frozen corn niblets
¹/₂ cup frozen peas
1 Tbsp minced parsley

Heat the oil in a large saucepan and add the carrot, turnip, leeks, and potatoes. Sauté gently for about 10 minutes or until softened. Stir in the broth, tomatoes, bay leaf, savory or marjoram, soup pasta, salt, and pepper. Bring gently to a boil, reduce the heat, and simmer gently for 20 minutes.

Add the beans and okra and cook for a further 10 minutes. Finally add the corn, peas, and parsley. Cook for 5 minutes before serving.

Time: Preparation takes about 20 minutes, cooking takes about 45 minutes.

Cook's Tip: This recipe can be adapted for vegans by omitting the soup pasta and replacing it with brown rice.

Variation: Instead of using canned tomatoes use 6 fresh tomatoes and ²/₃ cup vegetable broth or water instead.

Salad Soup

A delicious, unusual soup that is as refreshing as its name implies.

SERVES 4-6

2-3 medium potatoes, peeled and diced
2 cups vegetable broth
6 green onions (scallions), finely chopped
½ head Boston or iceberg lettuce, washed and shredded
2 cups fresh spinach leaves, washed, trimmed, and shredded
1 bunch watercress, washed, trimmed, and chopped
½ cucumber, peeled and grated or diced
2½ cups milk
2 Tbsps minced fresh parsley
Pinch of nutmeg
Pinch of cayenne pepper
Salt and freshly ground black pepper
⅔ cup light cream
Natural yogurt and slices of cucumber, to garnish

Cook the potatoes in the broth for 15 minutes or until tender. Add all the remaining vegetables and cook for a further 5 minutes. Pour into a blender or food processor and purée until smooth. Return to the rinsed-out saucepan.

Stir in the milk and parsley and season with nutmeg, cayenne pepper, salt, and pepper. Add the cream and reheat gently, but do not allow to boil. Garnish with swirls of plain yogurt and slices of cucumber before serving.

Time: Preparation takes about 10 minutes, cooking takes about 25 minutes.

Green Pea Soup

Pale-green and creamy, this delicious soup is made with frozen peas, making it possible to enjoy the taste of summer all year round.

SERVES 4

2 Tbsp butter or margarine
1 shallot, minced
2 Tbsps all-purpose flour
1¼ cups vegetable broth
2 cups milk
1 pound frozen peas
¼ tsp dried marjoram
1 Tbsp chopped fresh parsley
Salt and freshly ground black pepper
1 small bunch fresh mint
⅔ cup light cream

Melt the butter or margarine in a saucepan and sauté the shallot until soft. Stir in the flour and cook gently for about 1 minute. Remove the pan from the heat and gradually add the broth and milk. Reserve about ½ cup of the peas and add the rest to the pan, along with the marjoram, parsley, and seasoning. Heat gently until slightly thickened. Pour the soup into a blender or food processor and blend until smooth.

Using a sharp knife, chop the mint very finely. Stir the mint, along with the cream, into the puréed soup. Stir in the reserved peas and reheat gently before serving.

Time: Preparation takes about 10 minutes, cooking takes about 15 minutes.

Parsnip & Carrot Soup

A delicious and wholesome country soup which makes good use of an unusual root vegetable, the parsnip. If it is not available, substitute jicama.

SERVES 4

2 parsnips, peeled and sliced
4 medium carrots, peeled and sliced
1¼ cups vegetable broth
2½ cups milk
Salt and freshly ground black pepper
Pinch of ground nutmeg
1 small bunch chives, snipped
4 Tbsps light cream

Cook the parsnips and carrots in the broth for about 15 minutes until tender. Place in a blender or food processor and purée until smooth. Return to the rinsed-out saucepan. Add the milk, season with salt, pepper, and nutmeg, and stir in the chives. Reheat gently until just simmering. Stir in the cream and serve.

Time: Preparation takes about 10 minutes, cooking takes about 20 minutes.

Serving Idea: Serve with crisp French bread and a vegetarian cheese.

Freezing: This soup will keep for up to 3 months if frozen before the final addition of the cream. This can be added just before serving.

Cheddar Cheese Soup

An unusual soup that is ideal for using up any leftover cheese.

SERVES 4

8 ounces vegetarian Cheddar cheese
3 Tbsps butter or margarine
1 carrot, peeled and diced
2 sticks celery, trimmed and chopped
2 Tbsps all-purpose flour
2 cups vegetable broth
2½ cups milk
1 bay leaf
¼ tsp dried thyme
Minced parsley, to garnish

Grate the cheese finely and, if using more than one type, mix together. Melt the butter or margarine in a pan and sauté the carrot and celery until just soft. Stir in the flour and cook for about 30 seconds. Remove from the heat and gradually add the broth and milk. Add the bay leaf and thyme. Return to the heat and cook gently until thickened slightly, stirring constantly.

Add the cheese a little at a time, stirring until it has melted. Remove the bay leaf and serve the soup sprinkled with minced parsley.

Time: Preparation takes about 10 minutes, cooking takes about 20 minutes.

Serving Idea: Serve with Jewish rye bread.

Sherry Cream Soup with — Mushrooms —

This unusual soup is hearty and filling, making it ideal for a cold day.

SERVES 4

2 pounds mushrooms, trimmed and chopped
5-6 slices stale bread, crusts removed
3 cups vegetable broth
1 sprig of fresh thyme
1 bay leaf
½ clove garlic, crushed
Salt and freshly ground black pepper
2 cups light cream
4 Tbsps sherry
2 cups whipped cream
Grated nutmeg, to garnish

Place the mushrooms in a large pan and crumble the bread over them. Add the broth, thyme, bay leaf, garlic, salt, and pepper. Bring to a boil, reduce the heat, and simmer gently for 20 minutes, or until mushrooms are soft, stirring occasionally.

Remove the bay leaf and thyme. Blend the soup to a smooth purée in a blender or food processor. Return to the rinsed-out pan. Whisk in the light cream and sherry. Reheat gently but do not allow to boil. Garnish each serving with a tablespoon of whipped cream and a sprinkling of nutmeg.

Time: Preparation takes 20 minutes, cooking takes 25 minutes.

Purée of Asparagus — Soup —

This thick and creamy soup makes full use of the delicate flavor of fresh summer asparagus.

SERVES 4

3 pounds asparagus, fresh or frozen and thawed
1 quart vegetable broth
¼ tsp ground mace or nutmeg
Salt and freshly ground black pepper
1¼ cups light cream
⅔ cup whipped cream
Sprinkling of ground mace or nutmeg

Trim the thick ends from the asparagus and cut away any tough outer skin. Chop the spears into 1-inch pieces. Bring the broth to a boil in a large pan, add the asparagus, mace, and seasoning, and cook for about 10 minutes or until asparagus is just tender.

Using a blender or food processor, blend the asparagus in the cooking liquid until it becomes a smooth purée. Return the asparagus to the rinsed-out pan and stir in the light cream. Reheat gently but do not allow to boil or the cream will curdle. Garnish each serving with a spoonful of the whipped cream and a dusting of the mace or nutmeg.

Time: Preparation takes about 15 minutes, cooking takes about about 15 minutes.

Serving Idea: Serve with slices of whole-wheat bread for a gourmet appetizer.

Creamy Spinach Soup

The wonderful combination of spinach and cream in this soup could not fail to please even the most demanding guest.

SERVES 4-6

2 pounds fresh spinach, trimmed and well washed
2 Tbsps butter or margarine
1 shallot, minced
2 Tbsps all-purpose flour
3 cups vegetable broth
¼ tsp dried marjoram
1 bay leaf
Pinch of grated nutmeg
Salt and freshly ground black pepper
Squeeze of lemon juice
2 cups milk
⅔ cup light cream
Slices of lemon or chopped hard-cooked egg, to garnish

Cook the spinach until just wilted in a covered saucepan with just the water that is left clinging to the leaves. Melt the butter or margarine in a large pan and sauté the shallot until soft. Stir the flour into the pan and cook for about 30 seconds. Remove from the heat and gradually add the broth. Add the marjoram, bay leaf, and nutmeg. Return to the heat and cook gently until thickened slightly, stirring constantly.

Remove and discard the bay leaf. Add the spinach to the pan. Season with salt and pepper and add the lemon juice. Purée the soup in a blender or food processor until smooth. Return to the rinsed-out pan and stir in the milk. Bring gently to simmering point. Stir in the cream just before serving. Serve garnished with lemon slices or chopped hard-cooked eggs.

Time: Preparation takes about 15 minutes, cooking takes about about 20 minutes.

Variation: Use a mixture of watercress and spinach for a tasty variation.

Serving Idea: Serve with crunchy whole-wheat croutons.

Freezing: This soup will freeze successfully for up to 3 months without the cream and garnish.

Fennel and Walnut Soup

A delicious and unusual combination of ingredients makes this soup perfect for special occasions.

SERVES 4

1 bulb fennel, chopped

1 head celery, chopped

1 large onion, chopped

1 Tbsp olive or sunflower oil

6 Tbsps walnuts, crushed

5 cups vegetable broth, bean broth, or water

3 Tbsps Pernod

⅔ cup light cream

Salt and freshly ground black pepper

Parsley to garnish

Sauté the fennel, celery, and onion in the oil over a low heat. Add the walnuts and broth and simmer for half an hour. Blend the simmered ingredients together and return to the pan. Add the Pernod, light cream, salt, and pepper. Reheat gently and serve garnished with parsley.

Time: Preparation takes about 15 minutes, cooking about 1 hour 10 minutes.

Serving Idea: Celery leaves or coriander (cilantro) may be used as a garnish instead of parsley.

Variation: Other nuts such as cashews or almonds may be used in place of walnuts.

Watchpoint: Do not allow the soup to boil after adding the cream and Pernod.

Miso Soup

This delicious soup of Japanese origin makes a nice change for an appetizer.

SERVES 2

1 small onion, grated

1-inch fresh root ginger, peeled and minced

1 clove garlic, crushed

1 tsp sesame oil

1 carrot, peeled and finely sliced

¼ small cauliflower, divided into flowerets

5 cups water

1 large Tbsp arame (Japanese seaweed)

2 Tbsps garden peas (fresh or frozen)

2 Tbsps shoyu (Japanese soy sauce)

1 Tbsp miso (red bean paste)

Freshly ground black pepper to taste

2 green onions (scallions), finely chopped

Sauté the onion, ginger, and garlic in the sesame oil for a few minutes. Add the carrot and cauliflower and gently sweat the vegetables for 5 minutes. Add the water, arame, peas, and shoyu. Cook for 15-20 minutes until the vegetables are soft. Blend the miso to a paste with a little of the soup liquid and add this to the soup, but do not allow to boil. Season with freshly-ground black pepper to taste. Serve garnished with chopped green onions (scallions).

Time: Preparation takes 15 minutes, cooking takes 20 minutes.

Serving Idea: Serve with hot garlic bread or Japanese buckwheat noodles. For an exotic garnish, try enoki mushrooms.

Tomato and Leek Soup

This delicious combination of leeks and sweet tomatoes is sure to become a firm favorite.

SERVES 4-6

2 large leeks, washed, trimmed, and finely sliced
2½ cups fresh tomato juice
Dash of Tabasco or soy sauce
¼ tsp celery seasoning
Dash of garlic powder
4 fresh tomatoes, skinned and sliced
Salt and freshly ground black pepper

Cook the leeks in about 1½ cups of boiling water for 15 minutes, or until tender. Remove about half the leeks from the cooking liquid and set aside. Purée the remaining leeks with the cooking liquid, in a blender or food processor. Return the puréed leeks to the rinsed-out pan and add another 1½ cups water. Stir in the tomato juice, Tabasco or soy sauce, celery seasoning, and garlic powder. Heat gently to simmering point then add the reserved leeks and tomato slices, and season with salt and pepper. Cook gently for 3-4 minutes and serve good and hot.

Time: Preparation takes about 10 minutes, cooking takes about about 20 minutes.

Serving Idea: Serve with crusty French bread and vegetarian Cheddar cheese.

Freezing: This soup will freeze for up to 6 weeks. Freeze in a rigid 2-quart container.

Gazpacho

One of Spain's tastiest exports is this refreshing, chilled soup.

SERVES 4

1 pound ripe tomatoes
1 small onion
1 small green bell pepper
1 clove garlic, crushed
½ cucumber
1 Tbsp red wine vinegar
1 Tbsp olive oil
14-ounce can tomato juice
1-2 Tbsps lime juice
Salt and freshly ground black pepper

Plunge the tomatoes into boiling water, leave for 2 minutes, then remove the skins and seeds. Chop the onion and pepper and place in a blender with the tomatoes, garlic, cucumber, vinegar, oil, and tomato juice. Purée until smooth. Add the lime juice and seasoning to taste. Pour the soup into a glass dish and chill until required.

Time: Preparation takes 10 minutes.

Serving Idea: Serve garnished with croutons and finely diced cucumber.

Watchpoint: If the soup is too thick, add more tomato juice after chilling.

Variation: Lemon juice may be used in place of the lime juice.

Split Pea Soup

A classic soup which looks extra special with a swirl of yogurt on top.

SERVES 6

1 cup split peas
3¾ pints vegetable broth
4 Tbsps butter or margarine
1 large onion, chopped
3 sticks celery, chopped
2 leeks, finely sliced
2 medium potatoes, peeled and diced
1 medium carrot, finely chopped
Salt and freshly ground black pepper

Cook the peas in the broth for 10-15 minutes. Meanwhile, melt the margarine and sauté the onion, celery, and leeks for a few minutes. Add to the peas and broth, together with the potatoes and carrot, and bring back to a boil. Simmer for 30 minutes. Season well and blend until smooth.

Time: Preparation takes about 10 minutes, cooking takes 40 minutes.

Serving Idea: If the vegetables are chopped small enough you can omit the blending and serve this as a chunky soup.

Cook's Tip: If you do not have a blender you can pass the soup through a sieve, although it will not be quite as thick.

French Onion Soup

This soup tastes best if cooked the day before it is needed and then reheated as required.

SERVES 4

3 medium onions
4 Tbsp butter or margarine
2 Tbsp all-purpose or soya flour
1 quart boiling vegetable broth
Salt and freshly ground black pepper
Topping
4 slices French bread, cut crosswise
4 Tbsps grated vegetarian Cheddar cheese
2 Tbsps grated vegetarian Parmesan cheese

Slice the onions very finely into rings. Melt the butter in a saucepan, add the onion rings, and fry over a medium heat until well browned. Mix in the flour and stir well until browned. Add the broth and seasoning and simmer for 30 minutes.

Toast the bread on both sides. Combine the cheeses, and divide between the bread slices; broil until golden-brown. Place the slices of bread and cheese in the bottom of individual soup dishes and spoon the soup over the top. Serve at once,

Time: Preparation takes 10 minutes, cooking takes 30 minutes.

Variation: For a special occasion, add a tablespoonful of brandy to the broth.

Watchpoint: The onions must be very well browned, as they give the soup its rich color.

Chestnut Soup

This unusual soup is high in protein and dietary fiber, and is so delicious that it will become a firm family favorite.

SERVES 4

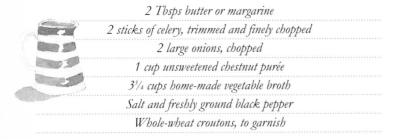

2 Tbsps butter or margarine

2 sticks of celery, trimmed and finely chopped

2 large onions, chopped

1 cup unsweetened chestnut purée

3¼ cups home-made vegetable broth

Salt and freshly ground black pepper

Whole-wheat croutons, to garnish

Melt the butter or margarine in a large saucepan and sauté the celery and onion until just soft. Blend the chestnut purée with a little of the broth and add to the pan along with the remaining broth. Season with salt and pepper. Bring gently to a boil, reduce the heat, and simmer gently for 35 minutes. Serve garnished with the croutons.

Time: Preparation takes about 15 minutes and cooking takes about 40 minutes.

Preparation: If unsweetened chestnut purée is unavailable, cook 1 cup shelled chestnuts in ⅔ cup boiling water until they are soft, and grind them in a blender or food processor.

Freezing: This soup will freeze for 1 month.

Beet & Sour Cream Soup

This delicious soup is worthy of any special occasion.

1 pound raw beets

4 small turnips, peeled and cut into even-sized pieces

1 quart vegetable broth

1 bay leaf

Salt and freshly ground black pepper

1¼ cups sour cream

1 Tbsp grated fresh or bottled horseradish

Snipped chives, to garnish

Boil the beets in salted water for about 30-40 minutes or until soft. (Large, older beets may take longer.) Remove from the pan and leave until cold enough to handle. Carefully remove the skins and any roots from the cooked beets, using a small knife. Cut the cooked beets into small pieces and put these, along with the turnips, broth, bay leaf, salt, and pepper, into a large saucepan. Bring to a boil, then reduce the heat and simmer gently for 20 minutes or until the turnip is tender. Remove the bay leaf and discard.

Using a blender or food processor, blend the soup until it becomes a smooth purée. Return to the rinsed-out pan. Reserve 4 tablespoons of the sour cream and stir the remainder into the soup along with the horseradish.

Reheat gently for a few minutes but do not allow the soup to boil. Serve the soup topped with the reserved cream and a sprinkling of snipped chives.

Time: Preparation takes about 20 minutes, cooking takes about 1 hour.

Freezing: This soup will freeze for up to 2 months.

Corn & Red Pepper Soup

This creamy soup has a definite bite in its flavor. It can be made with fresh or canned, white or yellow, corn kernels.

SERVES 4

4 medium potatoes, scrubbed and cut into even-sized pieces

1 bay leaf

2½ cups vegetable broth

1 Tbsp butter or margarine

1 onion, chopped

1 large red pepper, deseeded and chopped

1 red chili, chopped

1 cup corn kernels

2½ cups milk

Salt and freshly ground black pepper

Freshly chopped parsley, to garnish

Place the potatoes in a saucepan with the bay leaf and cover with the broth. Bring to a boil and simmer gently for 15 minutes or until tender. Remove the bay leaf, then pour the potatoes and broth into a blender or food processor and blend until smooth.

Melt the butter or margarine in another pan and add the onion, red pepper, and chili. Sauté gently for 5-10 minutes or until soft. Add the puréed potatoes to the pan, along with the sweetcorn and milk, and stir to blend thoroughly. Reheat gently and season to taste. Serve garnished with chopped parsley.

Variation: If preparing this soup for vegans, substitute soya milk for fresh milk, but do not boil the soup after this addition, and use non-dairy margarine.

Time: Preparation takes about 20 minutes, cooking takes about about 30 minutes.

Serving Idea: Serve with fresh, crusty rolls.

Cook's Tip: Great care must be taken when preparing fresh chilies. Use clean rubber gloves and do not get the juice near eyes or mouth. Rinse eyes with lots of clear cold water should you accidently get juice in them.

Appetizers

Newcomers to vegetarian cookery, faced with the prospect of preparing a three-course meal, might well fall at the first hurdle! Finding a suitable first course recipe for a dinner party may seem like a problem, but in practice there are plenty of ingredients that can be transformed into tempting appetizers to get any meal off to a good start.

Pâtés might well have unacceptable connotations, but surprisingly good pâtés can be prepared from a base of vegetables, with creamy tofu, beans, or even nuts to add extra body. The classic hummus, made from puréed, cooked chickpeas is one starter which is acceptable to all, vegetarian or not. Hummus (p. 37) and other simple dipping textured pâtés and spreads make informal appetizers, perfect for serving with raw vegetables sticks for dipping or dainty squares of melba toast or strips of pita bread.

Attractively arranged salads also make a good choice for a first course. Adding unusual ingredients to the more familiar salads will give an unexpected twist, while for a really impressive result try serving them with a home-made dressing. Arrange on the plate just before serving for maximum freshness.

Many first course favorites are served cold, but there is no reason why even elements of a salad couldn't be hot – just watch out for overcooking. Freshness and maximum visual appeal underlie the success of an appetizer to set the tone for a meal. Dishes requiring a minimum of cooking are ideal – just a brief heating time to ensure that the cook doesn't spend too long in the kitchen.

For vegetarian cooks, small vegetables can make perfect centerpieces for appetizers. Although stuffed mushrooms are something of a cliché, bell peppers, eggplant, artichokes, and tomatoes all make excellent subjects for savory stuffing mixtures.

Choose dishes with an exciting spiciness or strong flavor to really whet the appetite. It's no wonder that garlic features so frequently in favorite appetizer recipes. The wonderful aroma easily escapes from the kitchen to entice and encourage digestive juices to flow. By the time garlic mushrooms or garlic bread hit the table, guests are more than ready to get started.

Appetizer portions should never be too large, though – there's nothing more frustrating for a host or hostess than to reach the entrée stage, only to find everyone's appetite has been satiated already. Smaller plates help make a little appear more, and particularly hungry eaters can always fill up with extra bread if they really can't wait for the next dish!

Watercress & Mushroom Pâté

A delightful pâté, garnished with lime or lemon wedges and served with thinly sliced, buttered brown bread.

SERVES 4

2 Tbsp butter or margarine
1 medium onion, minced
6 dark, flat mushrooms, finely chopped
1 bunch watercress, finely chopped
½ cup low fat small-curd cottage cheese
Few drops of shoyu sauce (Japanese soy sauce)
Scant ½ tsp caraway seeds
Freshly ground black pepper

Melt the butter over a low heat and cook the onion until soft but not colored. Raise the heat, add the mushrooms, and cook quickly for 2 minutes. Add the chopped watercress and stir for about 30 seconds, until it becomes limp.

Place the contents of the pan in a blender together with the cheese and shoyu sauce. Blend until smooth. Stir in the caraway seeds and pepper to taste. Put into individual ramekin dishes or one large serving dish and chill for at least 2 hours until firm.

Time: Preparation takes 10 minutes, cooking takes 5 minutes.

Cook's Tip: It may be necessary to stir the contents of the blender several times as the mixture should be fairly thick.

Bean Fiesta

If dried flageolet beans are hard to find, use lima beans

SERVES 4

1 cup dried flageolet beans, soaked overnight, soaking water discarded
1 medium onion
1 clove garlic
1 small cucumber
2 Tbsps chopped parsley
2 Tbsps chopped mint
2 Tbsps olive oil
Grated rind and juice of 1 lemon
Salt and freshly ground black pepper
Watercress to garnish

Cook the flageolet beans in plenty of fresh, boiling water for about 1 hour or until just tender. Drain and put into a mixing bowl. Peel and mince the onion. Crush the garlic and chop the cucumber into bite-sized pieces. Add the onion, garlic, cucumber, herbs, oil, lemon juice, and rind to the beans and mix well. Add seasoning to taste and leave to marinate for 2 hours. Transfer to a clean serving bowl. Serve garnished with watercress.

Time: Preparation takes 15 minutes. Marinating takes 2 hours and cooking takes 1 hour.

Serving idea: Serve with specialty breads or rolls as a picnic dish.

Indonesian-Style Stuffed — Peppers —

For this adaptable recipe you can substitute pine nuts or peanuts if you don't have cashews.

SERVES 8

2 Tbsps olive oil

1 medium onion, chopped

1 clove garlic, crushed

2 tsps turmeric

1 tsp crushed coriander (cilantro) seed

2 Tbsps unsweetened shredded coconut

1 cup chopped mushrooms

⅓ cup bulgar wheat

4 Tbsps raisins

2 Tbsps creamed coconut

1¼ cups broth or water

4 tomatoes, skinned and chopped

2 Tbsps cashew nuts

4 small green bell peppers, cut in half lengthwise

2 tsps lemon juice

Broth for cooking

Heat the oil and fry the onion and garlic until lightly browned. Add the turmeric, coriander (cilantro) seeds, and coconut and cook gently for about 2 minutes. Add the mushrooms and bulgar wheat and cook for a further 2 minutes. Add the rest of the ingredients except the nuts, lemon juice, peppers, and broth, and simmer gently for 15-20 minutes, until the bulgar wheat is cooked.

Toast the cashew nuts in a dry skillet until golden-brown. Blanch the peppers in boiling water for 3 minutes. Mix the nuts and lemon juice with the rest of the ingredients (except the broth) and fill the peppers with the mixture. Place the filled peppers in a large casserole dish and pour broth around the peppers. Bake in an oven preheated to 350 degrees for 20 minutes. Drain the peppers and place on a hot plate to serve.

Time: Preparation takes 20 minutes, cooking takes 45 minutes.

Freezing: The cooked peppers will freeze well for up to 3 months.

Spicy Hot Grapefruit

This simple dish makes an ideal appetizer, or even a refresher between courses.

SERVES 4

2 ruby grapefruits
1 tsp ground allspice
2 tsps superfine sugar (optional)
Lemon balm or mint leaves, to decorate

Cut the grapefruits in half. Using a small, sharp, serrated knife or a grapefruit knife, cut around the edges of each half between the flesh and the white parts. Carefully cut down between each segment and inner thin skins. Take hold of the white core and gently twist to remove, at the same time pulling away the thin inner skins which have been cut away from the grapefruit segments. Remove any seeds. Sprinkle each grapefruit half with equal amounts of the allspice and sugar, if using.

Place under a medium, preheated broiler for 3-4 minutes to heat through. Garnish with lemon balm or mint leaves.

Time: Preparation takes about 15 minutes, cooking takes about 5 minutes.

Preparation: The grapefruit halves can be prepared well in advance. Cover closely with plastic wrap to prevent drying out.

Variation: Sprinkle each grapefruit with ground ginger instead of the allspice and pour a teaspoon of ginger syrup or bourbon over each half.

Cauliflower and Broccoli
— Soufflettes —

Serve as a winter-time appetizer.

SERVES 6

1½ cups cauliflower flowerets
1½ cups broccoli flowerets
4 Tbsps butter or margarine
4 Tbsps brown rice flour
2 cups milk
4 Tbsps grated vegetarian Cheddar cheese
1 large egg, separated
Good pinch of grated nutmeg

Boil or steam the cauliflower and broccoli flowerets until just tender – about 6-8 minutes. Melt the margarine, remove from the heat, and gradually add the flour. Stir to a roux and add the milk gradually, blending well to ensure a smooth consistency. Return the pan to the heat and stir until the sauce thickens and comes to a boil. Cool a little, and add the egg yolk and cheese. Stir well and add nutmeg to taste. Whip the egg white until stiff and fold it carefully into the sauce.

Place the vegetables in 6 buttered individual ovenproof dishes and season. Divide the sauce evenly between the dishes and bake in an oven preheated to 375 degrees for about 35 minutes, until puffed and golden. Serve at once.

Time: Preparation takes 15 minutes, cooking takes 50 minutes.

Mixed Nut Balls

This versatile dish can be made in advance and
refrigerated until required for cooking.

SERVES 8

6 Tbsps ground almonds
6 Tbsps ground macadamias
6 Tbsps ground pecans
6 Tbsps whole-wheat bread crumbs
½ cup grated vegetarian Cheddar cheese
1 egg, beaten
4-5 Tbsps dry sherry or 2 Tbsps milk and 3 Tbsps dry sherry
1 small onion, minced
1 Tbsp grated fresh ginger
1 Tbsp chopped fresh parsley
1 small red or green chilli, finely chopped
1 medium red pepper, diced
1 tsp each salt and freshly ground black pepper

Mix the almonds, macadamias, and pecans together with the
bread crumbs and the cheese. In another bowl, mix the
beaten egg with the sherry, onion, ginger, parsley, chili, and red
pepper. Combine with the nut mixture and add the salt and
pepper. If the mixture is too dry, add a little more sherry or milk.
Form into small 1-inch balls. Do not preheat the oven. Arrange
the balls on a well-greased baking tray and bake at 350 degrees for
about 20-25 minutes, until golden-brown.
Time: Preparation takes about 20 minutes, cooking takes 20-25
minutes.

Parsnip Fritters

These tasty fritters make a nice change for lunch
or a light snack. If parsnips are not available, use rutabaga.

SERVES 4

1 cup all-purpose flour
2 tsps baking powder
1 tsp salt
½ tsp pepper
1 egg
⅔ cup milk
1 Tbsp melted butter
1½ pounds parsnips, cooked and finely diced
Oil or clarified butter for frying

Sift together the flour, baking powder, salt, and pepper. Beat
the egg and mix with the milk and melted butter. Stir this
mixture into the dry ingredients. Stir in the cooked parsnips.

Divide the mixture into
16 and shape into small
fritters. Fry in oil or
clarified butter until
browned on both sides.
Time: Preparation takes 10
minutes, cooking takes about 5-8 minutes per batch.
Variation: Zucchini, corn, onions, or eggplant may be substituted
for a root vegetable.
Serving Idea: Serve with yogurt sauce or make the fritters slightly
larger and serve as an entrée with salad.

Crudités

A great favorite when served with delicious dips.

SERVES 6-8

Choose from the following vegetable selection:

Cauliflower, broccoli – divided into flowerets

Carrots, celery, zucchini, cucumber – cut into matchstick pieces

Endive – separate the blades

Store or wild mushrooms – sliced or quartered

Peppers, daikon, kohlrabi, fennel, jicama – sliced

Baby radishes, green onions (scallions), cherry tomatoes – leave whole

Tomato and cheese dip

1 Tbsp butter or margarine

1 Tbsp grated onion

6 tomatoes, skinned and diced

4 Tbsps grated Cheddar cheese

4 Tbsps bread crumbs

1 egg, beaten

½ tsp dry mustard powder

Salt and freshly ground black pepper

2-4 Tbsps thick-set plain yogurt

Creamed curry dip

1 Tbsp mango chutney

6 Tbsps home-made or best quality mayonnaise

1 tsp curry paste

2 Tbsps heavy cream

Pinch of ground cumin

Avocado dip

2 ripe avocados

1 onion, diced

½ clove garlic, crushed

2 Tbsps lemon juice

Salt and freshly ground black pepper

Tomato and Cheese Dip

Melt the butter and gently fry the onion for 2 or 3 minutes until soft. Add the tomatoes, cover, and simmer for 10 minutes. Add the cheese, bread crumbs, and egg, and cook for a further minute, stirring all the time, until thickened. Do not allow to boil. Add the mustard and seasoning and blend or liquidize until smooth. Mix in enough yogurt to ensure a smooth "dipping" consistency and refrigerate until required.

Creamed Curry Dip

Chop the pieces of mango with a sharp knife and place in a bowl. Add the other ingredients and mix well. Refrigerate until required.

Avocado Dip

Peel the avocados, remove the stones, and chop the flesh roughly. Process or liquidize together with the onion, garlic, and lemon juice until smooth. Season to taste and refrigerate until required.

Time: Preparation takes 30 minutes, cooking takes 15 minutes.

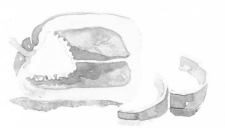

Stuffed Tomatoes Provençal

A refreshing appetizer, ideal as a first course to a rich meal.

SERVES 4

4 large ripe tomatoes
2 Tbsps butter or margarine
1 clove garlic, crushed
1 shallot, minced
1 cup finely chopped mushrooms
1 Tbsp white wine or vegetable broth
⅓ cup fresh white bread crumbs
1 tsp chopped fresh parsley
1 tsp chopped fresh basil
¼ tsp dried thyme
1 tsp Dijon-style mustard
Salt and freshly ground black pepper

Cut the tops off the tomatoes and carefully scoop out the flesh and seeds. Place in a sieve and strain off excess juice. Chop the flesh.

Melt the butter or margarine in a saucepan and sauté the garlic and shallot until soft. Stir in the mushrooms and wine or broth and cook gently for 4 minutes. Remove from the heat and stir in the bread crumbs, herbs, mustard, seasoning, and tomato flesh, mixing well. Fill each tomato with the mixture and place in a shallow ovenproof dish. Place caps on top. Bake in an oven preheated to 350 degrees, for 10 to 12 minutes. Serve hot.

Time: Preparation takes about 15 minutes, cooking takes about about 15 minutes.

Cee Jay Ratatouille

Cee Jay Ratatouille can be made in advance and reheated before covering with the apples.

SERVES 6

1 medium onion, thinly sliced
3 cloves garlic, crushed
4 Tbsps olive oil
1 large eggplant, diced
1 large red pepper, sliced
2 medium zucchini, sliced
4 medium tomatoes, sliced
1 tsp oregano
Salt and freshly ground black pepper
2 large dessert apples, thinly sliced
2 Tbsps butter or margarine
Ground cloves

Sauté the onion and garlic in the oil until the onion is transparent. Add the eggplant, pepper, zucchini, and tomatoes. Cook for a further 5 minutes, stirring occasionally. Add the oregano and seasoning and simmer, covered, for 15-20 minutes.

Divide the ratatouille between 6 heated ovenproof dishes and cover each one with a layer of thinly sliced apple. Melt the butter or margarine and brush over the top of the apples. Sprinkle with a good pinch of ground cloves and broil until the apples are browned and fluffy. Serve immediately.

Time: Preparation takes 15 minutes, cooking takes 30 minutes.

Cook's Tip: This dish can be kept warm in a moderate oven for up to 30 minutes.

Asparagus and Orange — Hollandaise —

Simplicity is often the making of a classic dish, and serving fresh asparagus in this way is certainly a classic combination.

SERVES 4

2 pounds asparagus spears
Grated rind and juice of ½ orange
Juice of ½ lemon
1 bay leaf
Blade of mace
4 Tbsps butter
3 egg yolks, beaten
Salt and freshly ground black pepper
Strips of blanched orange rind, to garnish (optional)

Trim away any thick, tough ends from the asparagus and rinse them well. Bring a sauté pan of lightly salted water to a boil. Move the pan so that it is half on and half off the direct heat (take care not to spill the water). Place the asparagus in the pan so that the tips are in the part of the pan off the direct heat. Cover the pan and bring back to a boil. Cook the asparagus for about 10 minutes or until just tender; drain and keep warm.

Meanwhile, prepare the sauce. Heat the orange juice, lemon juice, bay leaf, and mace in a small pan to almost boiling and allow to stand for a few moments. Melt the butter in the top of a double boiler or in a bowl placed over a pan of gently simmering water. Whisk the beaten egg yolks into the butter and add the orange rind. Strain the juice into the butter and egg mixture and whisk well. Cook gently until the sauce thickens, whisking constantly. As

soon as the sauce has reached the desired consistency, remove it from the heat and stand the pan or bowl in cold water to prevent further cooking.

Arrange the asparagus on serving plates and pour equal amounts of sauce over each serving. Garnish with strips of orange rind if wished.

Time: Preparation takes about 10 minutes, cooking takes about 15 minutes.

Serving Idea: Serve with thin slices of whole-wheat bread.

Brazilian Avocados

The perfect way to impress your dinner guests right from the first course.

SERVES 4

2 large, ripe avocados
A little lemon juice
Salt and freshly ground black pepper
4 Tbsps finely chopped Brazil nuts
2 Tbsps grated vegetarian Cheddar cheese
2 Tbsps grated vegetarian Parmesan cheese
2 Tbsps minced fresh parsley
2 firm ripe tomatoes, skinned and finely chopped
Whole-wheat bread crumbs
2 Tbsps melted butter
A little paprika

Halve the avocados and carefully remove the flesh from the skins. Brush the inside of the skins with a little of the lemon juice. Dice the avocado and put it into a bowl with a sprinkling of lemon juice and the seasoning. Add the nuts, cheese, parsley, and tomato. Mix gently. Spoon the filling into the avocado shells, sprinkle with the bread crumbs and drizzle the butter over the top. Dust with the paprika and bake in an oven preheated to 400 degrees, for 15 minutes.

Time: Preparation takes about 10 minutes, cooking takes 15 minutes.

Cook's Tip: Do not prepare this dish too far in advance as the avocado may discolor.

Serving Idea: Serve as an entrée with a little salad as an appetizer or with baked potatoes, vegetables, and tossed green salad.

Celeriac à la Moutarde

This delicious appetizer could also be served as a light lunch or late dinner for two.

SERVES 4

1 large celeriac (celery root), peeled
4 Tbsps butter or margarine
2 Tbsps all-purpose flour
2½ cups milk
4 Tbsps Dijon mustard
1 tsp celery seasoning
Freshly ground black pepper
4 Tbsps dry bread crumbs

Cut the celeriac into ¼-inch thick slices and then into sticks about 1 inch long. Cook in lightly salted, boiling water for about 20 minutes or until just tender, then drain.

Meanwhile, melt 3 Tbsps of the butter or margarine in a saucepan. Stir in the flour and cook for about 30 seconds. Remove from the heat and gradually add the milk, stirring well after each addition. Return to the heat and stir in the mustard, celery seasoning, seasoning, and pepper. Cook gently until thickened, stirring constantly. Add the celeriac to the sauce and stir to coat well. Transfer it to a serving dish and keep warm. Melt the remaining butter or margarine in a small skillet and fry the bread crumbs until golden. Sprinkle the crumbs over the celeriac and serve immediately.

Time: Preparation takes about 10 minutes, cooking takes about 30 minutes.

Mushroom & Artichoke Salad

Wild mushrooms are becoming more readily available, and this recipe provides a delightful way of serving them.

SERVES 4

2-3 artichokes, depending on size

1 slice of lemon

1 bay leaf

6 black peppercorns

2 cups mixed wild mushrooms, e.g. shiitake or oyster

2 Tbsps vegetable oil

Radicchio, iceberg lettuce, and watercress leaves, mixed

2 Tbsps snipped fresh chives

6 Tbsps olive oil

2 Tbsps white wine vinegar

1 Tbsp Dijon mustard

Salt and freshly ground black pepper

Sprigs fresh dill or chervil, to garnish

Trim the pointed leaves from the artichokes with a sharp knife. Remove the stem. Place the lemon slice, bay leaf, and peppercorns in a saucepan of water and bring to a boil. Add the artichokes and cook for 30-40 minutes or until tender, when the bottom leaves should pull away easily. Stand each artichoke upside-down to drain completely.

Slice the mushrooms. Heat the vegetable oil in a skillet and fry the mushrooms for 5 minutes, or until just tender. Set aside. Tear the salad leaves into small pieces and place in a bowl with the snipped chives. Whisk together the olive oil, vinegar, mustard, and seasoning until thick and pale-colored. Remove the leaves from the drained artichokes and arrange them attractively on plates.

Time: Preparation takes about 20 minutes, cooking time is about 40 minutes.

Preparation: The mushrooms and artichokes can be prepared well in advance and kept in the refrigerator until required.

Fennel and Orange — Croustade —

A delicious mixture which is simple to prepare.

SERVES 4

4 x 1-inch-thick slices whole-wheat bread
Oil for deep-frying
2 fennel bulbs (reserve any fronds)
4 oranges
1 Tbsp olive oil
Pinch of salt
Chopped fresh mint for garnishing

Trim the crusts off the bread and cut into 3-inch squares. Hollow out the middles, leaving evenly shaped cases. Heat the oil and deep-fry the bread until golden-brown. Drain the bread well on absorbent kitchen paper. Leave to cool. Trim the fennel bulbs and slice thinly. Place in a mixing bowl. Remove all the peel and white parts from the oranges and cut into segments – do this over the mixing bowl to catch the juice.

Mix the orange segments with the fennel. Add the olive oil and salt and mix together thoroughly. Just before serving, divide the fennel and orange mixture evenly between the bread cases and garnish with fresh mint and fennel fronds.

Time: Preparation takes 15 minutes, cooking takes 5 minutes.

Variation: Serve the salad on individual plates sprinkled with croutons.

Cook's Tip: The salad can be made in advance and refrigerated until required but do not fill the cases until just before serving.

Bulgar Boats

This pretty appetizer can easily be taken on picnics.

SERVES 6

½ cup green lentils
½ cup bulgar
1 red bell pepper
1 green bell pepper
1 medium onion
2 Tbsps pine nuts (dry-roasted in a skillet)
2 tsps dried salad herbs (tarragon, chives, or parsley)
Juice and rind of 1 lemon
Salt and freshly ground black pepper
Romaine lettuce to serve

Remove any grit or stones from the lentils and rinse well. Cover with plenty of water and boil for about 20 minutes – do not overcook. Place the bulgar wheat in a mixing bowl and cover with boiling water. Leave for about 10 minutes – the grain will then have swollen, softened, and absorbed the water.

Dice the peppers and mince the onion. Drain the lentils and add to the wheat, together with the peppers, nuts, onion, herbs, lemon juice and rind, salt, and pepper. Using one large lettuce leaf per person, spoon the salad into the center of the leaves and arrange on a large serving platter garnished with wedges of lemon.

Time: Preparation takes 15 minutes, cooking takes 20 minutes.

Variation: Cashews or peanuts could be used instead of pine nuts.

Broccoli and Hazelnut Terrine

This colorful, crunchy terrine is full of protein and flavor.

SERVES 6-8

6-8 large whole spinach leaves
1 pound broccoli
2 eggs, beaten
¾ cup low-fat small-curd cottage cheese
1¼ cups heavy cream, lightly whipped
4 slices white bread, crusts removed, made into crumbs
1 shallot, minced
Pinch of dried thyme
Pinch of ground nutmeg
Salt and freshly ground black pepper
4 Tbsps hazelnuts, lightly toasted, then finely chopped
1¼ cups mayonnaise
⅔ cup plain yogurt
Grated rind and juice of 1 lemon
Pinch of cayenne pepper

Trim away any coarse stalks from the spinach, taking care to leave the leaves whole. Wash the leaves, blanch in boiling water for 1 minute, drain, and refresh in cold water. Drain again and pat dry.

Leaving at least 2 inches of leaf hanging over the edges, carefully line a 2-pound loaf pan with the spinach leaves. Overlap each leaf slightly to ensure that no gaps appear when the terrine is turned out.

Chop the broccoli finely. Put the eggs, cheese, cream, bread crumbs, shallot, thyme, nutmeg, salt, and pepper into a bowl and combine well. Stir in the broccoli and hazelnuts, mixing well to combine thoroughly. Spoon the mixture into the lined loaf pan, packing it down well, but taking care not to dislodge the spinach leaves. Carefully fold the spinach over the top of the terrine mixture. Cover with a sheet of nonstick baking parchment and then cover with foil. Place in a roasting pan and add enough hot water to come halfway up the sides of the loaf pan. Bake in a preheated oven at 325 degrees, for 1 hour, or until the terrine feels firm to the touch.

Cool the terrine completely, and chill before unmolding. In a bowl, mix together the mayonnaise, yogurt, lemon rind and juice, cayenne pepper, and a little salt. Serve the slices of the terrine coated with the sauce.

Time: Preparation takes about 20 minutes, cooking takes about 1 hour.

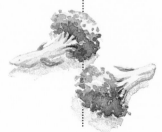

Date, Apple & Celery —Appetizer—

A healthy dish with a tasty mix of flavors.

SERVES 4

4 tsps unsweetened shredded coconut
2 crisp dessert apples
3-4 sticks celery
8 dates
2 Tbsps plain yogurt
Salt and freshly ground black pepper
Pinch of nutmeg

Toast the coconut in a dry skillet over a low heat until it is golden-brown, then put to one side. Core and dice the apples and chop the celery finely. Plunge the dates into boiling water, drain, and chop finely.

Combine the apples, celery, and dates in a mixing bowl. Add the yogurt, seasoning, and nutmeg and mix thoroughly so that the salad is coated completely. Transfer to a serving bowl and garnish with the toasted coconut. Serve at once.

Time: Preparation takes 10 minutes, cooking takes 2-3 minutes.
Serving Idea: Serve individual portions on a bed of watercress.
Cook's Tip: Red-skinned apples add color to this salad.

Hummus

A classic appetizer which also makes the perfect snack.

SERVES 4

1 cup cooked chickpeas (cooking liquid reserved)
4 Tbsps light tahini
Juice of 2 lemons
6 Tbsps olive oil
3-4 cloves garlic, crushed
Salt to taste

Put the cooked chickpeas into a blender together with ⅔ cup of the reserved broth. Add the tahini, lemon juice, half of the olive oil, garlic, and salt. Blend until smooth, adding a little more broth if it is too thick. Leave to stand for an hour or so, to let the flavors develop.

Serve on individual dishes with the remaining olive oil drizzled over the top.

Time: Preparation takes 10 minutes, standing time takes 1 hour.
Serving Idea: Serve sprinkled with paprika and garnished with wedges of lemon.

Salads & Light Entrées

Salads are no longer confined to seasonal supplies of home-grown lettuce, cucumber, and tomato. A huge array of fresh ingredients is now available all the year round to make crisp, colorful salads a permanent feature on everyone's menu. Farmers' markets and supermarkets are bursting with a wide variety of salad leaves and other greens, to make the basis of lovely salad bowls – and never has there been a wider choice of tomatoes, from the tiniest cherry to the plump plum variety. Add to these any number of different fresh vegetables, fruits, and herbs, raw or lightly cooked, and the scope for salads has never been greater.

With the growing acceptance of the importance of fresh fruit and vegetables in the diet, the inclusion of salad in the daily diet makes sound health sense. For more substantial salads, add cooked beans or lentils, grains, nuts, cheese (especially feta or blue cheese) or eggs, to turn a side-dish into an entrée.

The choice of dressing can also change the character of a salad. There is a good choice of commercial salad dressings available from shops and these do save time, but for regular salad eaters, it's worthwhile investing in a quality salad oil and one or two specialty vinegars, to enable you to experiment with basic dressing recipes. The foundation of a good salad dressing is a good quality oil. Virgin oils are obtained from a plant's first pressing, giving the best flavor, and not surprisingly these are the priciest. Good quality virgin olive oil is a perfect basis for dressings, while specialty oils such as walnut, hazelnut, sesame, or almond add their own distinctive flavors. Vinegars too come in many different flavors, from the familiar cider and wine vinegars to the flavored vinegars and the expensive, balsamic vinegar, imported from Italy.

Always remember to dress leafy salads just before serving, but to toss hot ingredients in the dressing as soon as they are cooked, to allow flavors to be well absorbed. Salads can make wonderful light meals in themselves as can other dishes based on vegetables, such as the classic Ratatouille (p. 45), the humble baked potato, pasta dish, or risotto. There's plenty of scope for meals which bridge the gap between snack and entrée.

Greek Salad

A great favorite which has the added advantage of being easy to prepare.

SERVES 4

2 tomatoes
½ green pepper
¼ cucumber
2 sticks celery, finely sliced
1 tsp fresh basil, finely chopped
Few crisp leaves of lettuce
½ cup vegetarian Feta cheese, diced
16 black olives

Dressing
4 Tbsps olive oil
2 Tbsps lemon juice
1 clove garlic, crushed
Large pinch of oregano
Salt and freshly ground pepper

Cut each tomato into eight pieces and place in a large mixing bowl. Chop the pepper and cucumber roughly. Add this to the tomato, together with the celery and chopped basil. Mix together the oil, lemon juice, garlic, oregano, and seasoning, and pour over the salad. Mix well to coat all the vegetables.

Arrange a few leaves of lettuce in the bottom of a serving bowl and pile the salad on the top, followed by the cheese cubes. Garnish with olives.

Time: Preparation takes 15 minutes.

Serving Idea: Serve with pita bread.

Variation: Add a few croutons just before serving.

Fresh & Dried Beans — Provençale —

This attractive dish is full of flavor and is high in protein too.

1 cup dried pink or pinto beans, soaked
1 pound tomatoes, skinned and chopped
1 clove garlic, crushed
2 tsps dried basil
1 tsp dried oregano
½ tsp dried rosemary
1 pound fresh or frozen green beans, trimmed

Drain the beans and place in a saucepan with enough fresh water to cover them by 1 inch. Bring to a boil, boil rapidly for 10 minutes, then reduce the heat and simmer gently for 1-1½ hours or until the beans are soft. Drain and set aside until required.

Place the tomatoes, garlic, and herbs in a saucepan and cook over a low heat for 10 minutes or until the tomatoes soften and the juice begins to flow. Cut the green beans into 1-inch lengths and add to the pan along with the cooked flageolet beans. Cook gently for 15 minutes or until the flavors are well combined.

Time: Preparation takes about 15 minutes, plus about 3 hours soaking. Cooking takes about 2 hours.

Cook's Tip: Canned beans can be used and they will substantially reduce the overall cooking time dramatically. Use 1 pound canned, drained beans in this recipe.

Serving Idea: Serve this casserole over grits or cooked rice.

Smoked Tofu Salad

Serve this tasty main course salad with mixed grain bread.

SERVES 4-6

2 cups broccoli flowerets
1 cup mushrooms
4 canned pineapple rings
4 Tbsps corn kernels
4-6 Tbsps French dressing
1 package smoked tofu, cut into cubes

Cover the broccoli flowerets with boiling water and leave to stand for 5 minutes. Drain and allow to cool. Wipe the mushrooms with a clean cloth and slice thinly.

Cut the pineapple into small pieces. Put the broccoli, mushrooms, pineapple, and sweetcorn into a large bowl together with the French dressing. Mix carefully. Divide the salad between 4 individual dishes and place the smoked tofu on top. Serve at once.

Time: Preparation takes 15 minutes.

Variation: Omit the tofu and serve as a side-salad with a quiche.

Cook's Tip: Plain tofu can be used if smoked is not available. Marinate it for a few hours in equal parts of shoyu sauce and olive oil, with 1 crushed clove of garlic and 1 teaspoon of grated ginger.

Green Pepper Salad

Serve in individual dishes as an appetizer, accompanied by crusty brown bread or as a light lunch with bread and chunks of cheese.

SERVES 4-6

3 medium green bell peppers
3 medium tomatoes
2 medium onions
½ cup sprouted lentils
Black grapes for garnish
Dressing
4 Tbsps olive oil
2 Tbsps red wine vinegar
2 tsps ground cumin
½ tsp fresh coriander, chopped

Core and slice the peppers finely. Slice the tomatoes and onions. Arrange the peppers, tomatoes, and onions alternately on a round serving dish and sprinkle the lentil sprouts over the top. Mix all the ingredients for the dressing together well and pour over the vegetables. Cover, and leave to marinate for at least 1 hour at room temperature before serving. Just before serving, garnish with halved black grapes.

Time: Preparation takes 10 minutes. Standing takes 1 hour.

Cook's Tip: You can prepare this salad in advance and refrigerate until required but remove from the refrigerator 30 minutes before serving.

Pasta & Asparagus Salad

This elegant green salad is a wonderful way of making the most of asparagus, that most luxurious of vegetables.

SERVES 4

4 ounces tagliatelle
1 pound asparagus, trimmed and cut into 1-inch pieces
2 zucchini, cut into 2-inch sticks
2 Tbsps chopped fresh parsley
2 Tbsps chopped fresh marjoram
1 lemon, peeled and segmented
Grated rind and juice of 1 lemon
6 Tbsps olive oil
Pinch of sugar
Salt and freshly ground black pepper
Crisp lettuce leaves
Frisée leaves

Cook the pasta in plenty of lightly salted, boiling water for 10 minutes or as directed on the package. Drain and refresh in cold water. Drain again and leave to cool completely.

Cook the asparagus in lightly salted, boiling water for 4 minutes, then add the zucchini and cook for a further 3-4 minutes, or until the vegetables are just tender. Drain and refresh in cold water. Drain again and leave to cool. Pile the cooked pasta, vegetables, herbs, and lemon segments into a large bowl and mix together, taking care not to break up the vegetables.

Mix together the lemon rind and juice, oil, sugar, and salt and pepper, to make the dressing. Arrange the lettuce and frisée on serving plates. Just before serving, pour the dressing over the vegetables and pasta and toss to coat well. Pile equal quantities of the pasta salad into the center of the salad leaves and serve immediately.

Time: Preparation takes about 15 minutes, plus cooling, cooking time is about 20 minutes.

Cook's Tip: Put the ingredients for the dressing into a Mason jar and shake vigorously to blend thoroughly.

Lima Bean, Lemon and — Fennel Salad —

This interesting combination of textures and flavors makes an unusual lunch or supper dish.

SERVES 4

1 cup lima beans, soaked overnight
1 lemon
1 large bulb fennel, thinly sliced
4 Tbsps vegetable or soya oil
Pinch of sugar
Salt and freshly ground black pepper
Lettuce and radicchio leaves, to serve

Place the lima beans in a saucepan, add enough water to cover them by 1 inch, and bring to a boil. Boil rapidly for 10 minutes, reduce the heat, and simmer gently for about 2 hours or until the beans are tender. Drain well.

Pare the rind from the lemon, taking care not to include too much of the white parts. Cut the rind into very thin strips. Blanch the lemon rind for 5 minutes in boiling water, then remove with a slotted spoon and transfer to kitchen paper. Add the fennel to the water, reserving the green tops, and blanch for 2 minutes. The fennel should be just cooked but still crunchy to the bite. Squeeze the juice from the lemon and place in a bowl with the lemon rind strips, oil, sugar, and seasoning, and whisk well together with a fork. Chop the fennel tops and add to the dressing. Mix the cooked beans and fennel in a large bowl, then add the dressing and toss to coat. Serve on a bed of lettuce and radicchio leaves.

Time: Preparation takes about 10 minutes, plus soaking. Cooking takes about 2 hours.

Black-Eyed Pea and — Orange Salad —

This colorful salad has a fresh taste which is given a delicious peppery "bite" by the addition of watercress.

SERVES 4

1 cup black-eyed peas, soaked
1 bay leaf
1 slice of onion
Grated rind and juice of 1 orange
5 Tbsps olive or grapeseed oil
6 black olives, pitted and quartered
4 green onions (scallions), trimmed and chopped
2 Tbsps each chopped fresh parsley and basil
Salt and freshly ground black pepper
4 whole oranges
1 bunch watercress, washed

Place the beans, bay leaf, and onion slice into a saucepan, add enough water to cover by 1 inch, and bring to a boil. Boil rapidly for 10 minutes, reduce the heat, and simmer gently for about 50 minutes–1 hour, or until the beans are tender.

Put the orange rind, juice, and oil in a large bowl and whisk together with a fork. Stir in the olives, green onions (scallions), and herbs. Add the drained beans to the dressing and season. Mix thoroughly to coat the beans well. Peel and segment the oranges; chop the flesh of 3 of the oranges and add to the beans.

Arrange the watercress on plates and pile equal amounts of the bean-and-orange salad on top. Arrange the remaining orange segments on the plate and serve immediately.

Time: Preparation takes about 20 minutes, plus soaking. Cooking takes about 1 hour.

Mushroom Croquettes

These tasty croquettes are served with a lightly spiced cream sauce.

SERVES 4

3 Tbsps butter or vegetable margarine
2 shallots, peeled and finely chopped
1 cup mushrooms, finely chopped
3 Tbsps all-purpose flour
²/₃ cup milk
²/₃ cup fresh bread crumbs
1 tsp each chopped fresh parsley and thyme
1 free-range egg, beaten
Salt and freshly ground black pepper
Dry bread crumbs for coating
Oil for shallow frying
2 Tbsps dry vermouth or white wine
1¼ cups heavy cream
2 Tbsps green peppercorns in brine, drained
½ sweet red pepper, seeded and diced

Melt half the butter or margarine in a skillet and stir in 1 shallot and the mushrooms. Sauté for 5 minutes or until softened. Stir in 2 Tbsps of the flour and cook for 1 minute. Remove from the heat and gradually beat in the milk. Return to the heat and cook until thickened. Stir in the bread crumbs, parsley, thyme, and half the egg. Season and mix to form a thick paste. Add extra bread crumbs if it is too thin, and chill well.

Divide into 12 and shape into small ovals with lightly floured hands. Dip in the remaining egg and coat in dry bread crumbs. Shallow fry for 3 minutes on each side until golden. Meanwhile, heat the remaining fat and shallot in a pan until softened. Stir in the remaining flour, whisk in the vermouth or wine and cream. Season to taste. Cook until thickened slightly. Stir in the peppercorns and red pepper and cook for 1 minute. Serve with a little sauce poured over them.

Time: Preparation takes about 30 minutes, plus chilling.
Cooking takes about 10 minutes.
Vegetarian Suitability: This recipe is suitable for lacto-vegetarians.
Serving Idea: Serve with a watercress and orange salad.

Spinach Salad

Serve with a simple main course.

SERVES 4-6

1 pound spinach
1 medium red cabbage
1 medium onion
½ cup apricots
6 Tbsps French dressing
4 Tbsps shelled, toasted sunflower seeds

Wash the spinach and drain well. First remove the outer leaves and core, then slice the cabbage thinly. Slice the onion thinly and cut the apricots into slivers. Tear the spinach leaves into bite-sized pieces and put into a serving dish. Add the sliced cabbage, onion, and apricots. Pour the dressing over and tmixture and toss lightly. Sprinkle with sunflower seeds and serve.
Time: Preparation takes 15 minutes.
Watchpoint: Spinach leaves bruise easily, so take care when washing and tearing the leaves.
Cook's Tip: If using dried apricots, soak them beforehand in a little fruit juice.

Ratatouille

This delicious classic dish is equally good served hot or cold.

SERVES 4-6

1 large eggplant
Salt
2 Tbsps olive oil
1 large onion, thinly sliced
1 clove garlic, crushed
1 green pepper, thinly sliced
1 pound tomatoes, skinned and chopped
1 tsp chopped fresh thyme
2 tsps chopped fresh basil
Salt and freshly ground black pepper
Sprigs of fresh thyme, to garnish

Cut the eggplant in half lengthwise and score the cut surface in a diamond fashion with a sharp knife. Sprinkle liberally with salt and allow to stand for 30 minutes, to remove excess moisture. Rinse well and pat dry with kitchen paper. Cut the eggplant halves into thin slices.

Heat the oil in a large skillet and fry the onion and garlic until it begins to soften, but not brown. Add the pepper and eggplant and sauté for 5 minutes. Stir in the remaining ingredients and cook gently for 30 minutes. Adjust seasoning if required and serve hot or cold. Garnish with a sprig of fresh thyme.
Time: Preparation takes about 20 minutes, plus standing. Cooking takes about 50 minutes.

Stuffed Potatoes

An unusual way of serving this popular vegetable meal.

SERVES 4

4 large baking potatoes, scrubbed

4 eggs

4 Tbsps butter or margarine

½ cup button mushrooms, sliced

1 shallot, minced

1 Tbsp all-purpose flour

2 cups milk

4 Tbsps grated vegetarian Cheddar cheese

Pinch each of dry mustard powder and cayenne pepper

Salt and freshly ground black pepper

1 bunch watercress, chopped

Grated cheese, cayenne, and watercress, to garnish

Preheat the oven to 400 degrees. Prick the potatoes a few times with a fork and place them directly on the oven shelves. Bake for ¾-1 hour, or until soft when squeezed. Reduce the oven temperature to 325 degrees and keep potatoes warm.

Poach the eggs in gently simmering water for 3½-5 minutes until the white and yolk are just set. Remove from the pan and keep in cold water. Melt 1 tablespoon of the butter or margarine in a small skillet and sauté the mushrooms and shallot for 5 minutes, until just beginning to soften. Melt the remaining fat in another pan, stir in the flour, and cook for about 1 minute. Remove from the heat and gradually 1¼ cups of the milk, stirring well after each addition. Return to the heat and cook gently until sauce thickens. Stir in the cheese, and continue cooking until cheese melts. Add the mustard, cayenne, salt, and pepper.

When the potatoes are cooked, cut a slice off the top and scoop out the flesh with a spoon, leaving a border to form a firm shell. Put equal amounts of the mushroom mixture into each potato and top with a well-drained egg. Spoon the cheese sauce mixture over the top. Heat the remaining milk until almost boiling. Mash the potato flesh, then gradually beat in the hot milk and watercress. Pipe or spoon the potato over the sauce in the potato shell.

Sprinkle the top with a little extra cheese and return to the oven for 15 minutes to warm through. Serve garnished with cayenne and watercress.

Time: Preparation takes about 20 minutes, cooking takes about 1½ hours.

Serving Idea: Serve with coleslaw or any other salad.

Seeli Salad

Serve this attractive salad for a party or as part of a buffet.

SERVES 4-6

1 large red cabbage
1 green pepper, chopped
½ small pineapple, peeled and finely chopped
Segments from 2 medium oranges
6 green onions (scallions), finely chopped
3 sticks celery, chopped
⅔ cup hazelnuts or macadamias, roughly chopped
⅔ cup sprouted aduki beans
Dressing
½ cup mayonnaise
¼ cup thick-set plain yogurt
Salt and freshly ground black pepper

Remove any tough or discolored outer leaves from the cabbage. Remove the base so that the cabbage will stand upright, and cut about a quarter off the top. Using a sharp knife, scoop out the inside of the cabbage leaving ¼ inch for the shell. Set the shell aside.

Discard any tough pieces and shred the remaining cabbage very finely. Put the cabbage into a large bowl together with the pepper, pineapple, orange, green onions (scallions), celery, hazelnuts, and beans. Mix the mayonnaise, yogurt, and seasoning together and carefully fold into the vegetables and fruits.
Put the mixture into the cabbage shell and place on a serving dish garnished with parsley.
Time: Preparation takes 20 minutes.

Kensington Salad

Top this salad with a row of sliced strawberries or kiwi fruits.

SERVES 4-6

3 large mushrooms, thinly sliced
1 dessert apple, cut into chunks and sprinkled with lemon juice
2 celery sticks, cut into matchsticks
2 Tbsps walnut pieces
1 bunch watercress
Dressing
1 Tbsp mayonnaise
1 Tbsp thick-set plain yogurt
½ tsp herb mustard
A little lemon juice
Salt and freshly ground black pepper

Place the mushrooms, apple, celery, and walnuts in a bowl. Combine all the ingredients for the dressing and mix gently with the vegetables. Arrange the watercress on a flat dish or platter and mound the salad mixture on the top.
Time: Preparation takes about 10 minutes.
Variation: A medium bulb of fennel, finely sliced, could be used in place of the celery.

Wheat Berry Salad

This substantial salad dish provides an almost perfect protein balance.

SERVES 4

1 cup wheat berries, cooked
½ cup red kidney beans, cooked
3 medium tomatoes
4 green onions (scallions), chopped
2 sticks celery, chopped
1 Tbsp pumpkin seeds

Dressing
4 Tbsps olive or sunflower oil
2 Tbsps red wine vinegar
1 clove garlic, crushed
1 tsp grated fresh root ginger
1 tsp paprika
1 Tbsp shoyu (Japanese soy sauce)
Fresh or dried oregano, to taste
Freshly ground black pepper

Mix the salad ingredients together, reserving a few pumpkin seeds and green onions (scallions) for garnishing. Shake the dressing ingredients together in a Mason jar. Pour over the salad and mix gently.

Time: Preparation takes 20 minutes.

Serving Idea: Serve with a lettuce salad. Wheat berries also mix well with grated carrot and an orange dressing.

Cook's Tip: This salad keeps well so it can be made in advance and kept in the refrigerator until required.

Tabouleh

This is a traditional salad from the Middle East. The main ingredient is bulgar – partially cooked cracked wheat – which only needs soaking for a short while before it is ready to eat.

SERVES 6

175g-200g/6-7oz bulgar wheat
1 tsp salt
340ml/12fl oz boiling water
450g/1lb tomatoes, chopped
½ cucumber, diced
½ spring onions

Dressing
60ml/4 Tbsps olive oil
60ml/4 Tbsps lemon juice
2 Tbsps chopped fresh mint
15g/4 Tbsps chopped fresh parsley
2 cloves garlic, crushed

Mix the bulgar wheat with the salt, pour over the boiling water and leave for 15-20 minutes. All the water will then be absorbed. Mix together the ingredients for the dressing and pour over the soaked bulgar. Fold in lightly with a spoon. Leave for two hours or overnight in a fridge or cool place. Add the salad ingredients and serve.

Time: Preparation takes about 20 minutes, standing takes about 2 hours.

Cook's Tip: A few cooked beans can be added to make this dish more substantial.

Serving Idea: Serve with flans, cold pies and roasts.

Chickpeas and Bulgar Wheat

High in protein and flavor, this simple lunch dish is sure to become a family favorite.

1 Tbsp vegetable oil

2 small onions, peeled and chopped

1 red pepper, seeded and chopped

1 pound cooked chickpeas

½ cup bulgar wheat

½ cup tomato paste

1 quart vegetable broth or water

Onion rings, to garnish

Heat the oil in a saucepan and fry the onions and pepper until soft but not colored. Stir in the chickpeas and bulgar wheat. Stir in the tomato paste, then gradually add the broth or water.

Bring gently to a boil, cover, and simmer gently for 10-15 minutes, or until the bulgur wheat is tender and the liquid has been absorbed. Transfer to a serving dish and garnish with onion rings.

Time: Preparation takes about 10 minutes, cooking takes about 20 minutes.

Serving Idea: Serve with a crunchy carrot-and-peanut coleslaw.

Vegetarian Suitability: This recipe is suitable for vegans.

Cook's Tip: The chickpeas should be boiled for at least 30 minutes. As an alternative, use 1 pound canned chickpeas, which will require no pre-cooking.

Variation: Use green peppers in place of the red peppers in this recipe, and add ½ teaspoon chili powder for a spicy variation.

Bavarian Potato Salad

It is best to prepare this salad a few hours in advance to allow the potatoes to absorb the flavors.

SERVES 4-6

2 pounds tiny new potatoes

4 Tbsps olive oil

4 green onions (scallions, finely chopped

1 clove garlic, crushed

2 Tbsps fresh dill, chopped or 1 Tbsp dried dill

2 Tbsps wine vinegar

½ tsp sugar

Salt and freshly ground black pepper

2 Tbsps chopped fresh parsley

Wash the potatoes but do not peel them; place them in a pan, cover with water, and boil until just tender. Whilst the potatoes are cooking, heat the olive oil in a skillet and cook the green onions (scallions) and garlic for 2-3 minutes, until they have softened a little. Add the dill and cook gently for a further minute. Add the wine vinegar and sugar, and stir until the sugar melts. Remove from the heat and add a little seasoning. Drain the potatoes and pour the dressing over them while they are still hot. Allow to cool and sprinkle with the parsley before serving.

Time: Preparation takes 15 minutes, cooking takes 15 minutes.

Serving Idea: Serve with cold roasts.

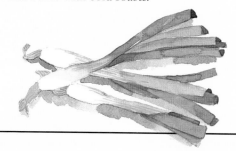

Red Lentil & Mushroom Loaf

This delicious and highly nutritious vegetable loaf is equally good served hot or cold.

SERVES 4-6

¾ cup red lentils

1½ cups vegetable broth or water

1 egg

2 Tbsps double cream

¾ cup mushrooms, chopped

½ cup small-curd cottage or cream cheese

1 clove garlic, crushed

1 Tbsp chopped fresh parsley

Salt and freshly ground black pepper

14-ounce can chopped tomatoes

1 Tbsp tomato paste

Pinch of sugar

1 Tbsp chopped fresh tarragon

Rinse the lentils and place in a saucepan with the broth or water. Bring gently to a boil, and boil rapidly for 10 minutes. Reduce the heat and continue to cook until the lentils are soft and the liquid has been absorbed.

Using a potato masher, mash the lentils to a thick purée. Beat the egg and cream together and add to the lentil purée, along with the mushrooms, cheese, garlic, parsley, and seasoning. Mix all the ingredients together thoroughly. Press the lentil mixture into a greased and lined 1 pound loaf pan. Bake in a preheated oven at 350 degrees for 1 hour or until firm to the touch.

Put the tomatoes, tomato paste, sugar, and half the tarragon into a small saucepan and cook for 5 minutes. Purée in a food processor or push through a sieve to form a smooth sauce.

Stir in the remaining tarragon and season to taste. Slice the loaf and serve with the tomato sauce and a mixed salad.

Time: Preparation takes about 15 minutes, cooking time is about 1 hour, 20 minutes.

Pasta and Avocado Salad

The perfect lunch or supper salad for guests.

SERVES 4

8 ounces pasta shapes

3 Tbsps mayonnaise

2 tsps tahini

1 orange

½ medium sweet red pepper, chopped

1 medium avocado

Pumpkin seeds (pepitas) to garnish

Cook the pasta until soft and leave to cool. Mix together the mayonnaise and tahini. Divide the orange into segments and chop into small pieces, retaining any juice. Chop the pepper. Stir the mayonnaise mixture, pepper, and orange (plus juice) into the pasta. Just before serving, cube the avocado and stir in carefully.

Serve decorated with pumpkin seeds (pepitas).

Time: Preparation takes about 10 minutes, cooking takes about 35 minutes.

Watchpoint: It is important not to peel the avocado until it is required, as it may discolor.

Variation: Green pepper may be used in place of the red pepper.

Vegetable Pilau

Lightly spiced and fragrant, this traditional Indian rice dish will serve 4 as a lunch or dinner entrée, or 6 as one of a selection of Indian dishes.

SERVES 4-6

4 Tbsps butter or vegetable oil

1 onion, finely sliced

1 cup long-grain rice

1 small piece cinnamon stick

4 cardamoms, husks removed and seeds crushed

4 cloves

½ tsp ground coriander

¼ tsp ground turmeric

¼ tsp garam masala

1 bay leaf

Salt and freshly ground black pepper

2½ cups pint vegetable broth or water

½ eggplant, diced

½ cup frozen cauliflower flowerets

½ cup frozen mixed vegetables

Melt the butter or heat the oil in a large saucepan and fry the onion until beginning to soften. Stir in the rice, spices, bay leaf, and seasoning and fry for 2 minutes, stirring constantly. Add the broth or water, stir well, bring gently to a boil and cook for 5 minutes. Add the remaining ingredients and cook for a further 5-7 minutes, or until rice is tender and most of the liquid has been absorbed. Leave covered for 5 minutes until the remaining liquid has been absorbed. Stir to separate the grains and serve.

Time: Preparation takes 10 minutes, cooking takes about 20 minutes.

Pancakes Provençale

These delicious pancakes are quick and easy to make.

SERVES 4

¼ cup all-purpose flour

Pinch salt

1 free-range egg

⅔ cup pint milk

Oil for frying

2 green peppers, seeded and diced

1 red pepper, seeded and diced

1 large onion, peeled and minced

1 clove garlic, crushed

1 small zucchini, diced

3 tomatoes, skinned, seeded, and chopped

1 tsp chopped fresh basil

2 Tbsps tomato paste

¼ cup vegetarian Colby or Monterey Jack cheese, crumbled

Salt and freshly ground black pepper

Fresh herbs and tomato slices, to garnish

Put the flour and salt into a bowl. Make a well in the center and add the egg and a little of the milk. Using a wooden spoon, gradually incorporate the flour into the egg mixture to form a smooth paste. Gradually beat in the remaining milk.

Heat a little oil in a heavy-based skillet and spoon in a little of the mix; swirl to coat the pan evenly. Cook for about 1 minute or until the underside of the pancake is golden. Flip or toss the pancake over and cook the other side. Slide the pancake out of the pan and keep warm. Repeat with the remaining batter. You should end up with 8 pancakes. Heat 2 tablespoons oil in a small pan and fry the peppers, onion and garlic until beginning to soften. Stir in the courgette and tomatoes and cook for 2 minutes. Add the basil, tomato purée, cheese and seasoning, and cook gently until cheese begins to melt.

Divide the vegetable mixture between the pancakes and roll or fold the pancakes to enclose the filling. Serve immediately garnished with sprigs of fresh herbs and tomato slices.

Time: Preparation takes about 20 minutes, cooking takes about 30 minutes.

Vegetarian Suitability: This recipe is suitable for lacto-vegetarians only. See variation for vegan alternative.

Variation: Omit the cheese from the filling and substitute halved pita pockets for the pancakes to make a vegan variation.

Spinach and Pepper
— Casserole —

This hearty, warm casserole makes a substantial lunch or supper dish, or could be used as an accompanying vegetable for up to 8 people.

1 pound spinach, washed, trimmed and roughly chopped

2 Tbsps oil

1 red bell pepper, seeded and sliced

1 green bell pepper, seeded and sliced

4 sticks celery, trimmed and thinly sliced

2 onions, peeled and minced

2 Tbsps yellow raisins

Pinch paprika

Pinch turbinado sugar

Pinch of ground cinnamon

Salt

2 Tbsps tomato paste

1 tsp cornstarch

2 Tbsps grated vegetarian Cheddar cheese

2 Tbsps fresh bread crumbs

Cook the spinach in a covered pan until wilted, with just the water that clings to the leaves after washing. Drain the spinach well, reserving the cooking liquid to make the sauce. Heat the oil in a skillet and fry the peppers, celery, and onions for about 10 minutes, or until softened.

Mix together the yellow raisins, paprika, sugar, cinnamon, salt, tomato paste, and cornstarch. Make the reserved cooking liquid up to ⅔ cup and stir into the cornstarch mixture. Add to the vegetables and cook, stirring until the sauce thickens. Spoon the vegetable mixture into a flameproof casserole dish. Mix together the cheese and bread crumbs and sprinkle over the vegetables. Place under a preheated broiler until the topping is golden.

Time: Preparation takes about 15 minutes, cooking time is about 20 minutes.

Vegetarian Suitability: This recipe is suitable for lacto-vegetarians only.

Serving Idea: Serve with a rice salad.

Entrées

Finding something to take the place of meat, fish, and fowl for the entrée of the main meal of the day is probably the biggest challenge facing those new to vegetarian eating. Vegetarian entrées, however, can be just as varied – and delicious – as any others. You can choose from a huge range of different plant foods – nuts, grains, beans, lentils, and seeds – and all kinds of fruits and vegetables, as well as dairy foods such as eggs, milk, yogurt, and cheese, where appropriate. There's no lack of raw materials and no shortage of tasty ways of preparing them either.

While vegetarian entrées beyond omelets and macaroni cheese may be quite a discovery, in many countries meat-free dishes have featured prominently for generations. Drawing on the traditions of India and the Orient, where vegetarianism is an integral feature of the cuisine, provides inspiration for many delicious dishes, such as Indian Vegetable Curry (p. 76), Sesame Stir-fry (p. 83) and Vegetable Couscous (p. 73).

Making more use of beans and lentils, grains, nuts, and seeds, all relatively rich in protein, is an important part of a balanced vegetarian diet. Simply replacing meat, fish, and fowl with more eggs and cheese results in a fat-rich diet. Dairy products are helpful, however, in boosting the protein intake of vegetarians. One of the keys to balancing a meat-free diet is to try to ensure that different protein foods are eaten together at a meal. That means mixing grains, nuts, seeds, beans, and lentils with each other or with dairy foods to make for a good balance of protein. Often this happens within a recipe – Nut and Herb Bulgar (p. 60), mixes nuts with bulgar, a wheat product, while Beany Lasagne (p. 79) combines beans with pasta, another wheat-based product. Pasta lends itself perfectly to vegetarian cooking – there's plenty of scope for serving pasta with traditional tomato-based sauces or dairy sauces, as well as experimenting with more contemporary recipes such as Pasta Spirals with Walnuts and Stilton (p. 66). Pastry dishes – quiches and pies – are also ideal for serving with a vegetarian filling and are often useful standbys to offer to those not familiar with vegetarian eating.

There are occasions when a straight substitute for a meat roast is required, and that's when the notorious nut roast comes into its own. The butt of many undeserving jokes, nut roasts should be given a fair chance to prove their delicious flavor. Blended from ground nuts, bread crumbs, and liberal use of herbs, seasonings, and often finely chopped vegetables, recipes such as Carrot and Cashew Nut Roast (p. 85) or Festive Roast (p. 85) could surprise and impress even die-hard meateaters.

Quick Vegetable Chili

Serve this tasty chili with whole-wheat rolls and salad.

SERVES 4

2 large onions, sliced
1 Tbsp olive oil
3-4 cloves garlic, crushed
1 tsp chili powder
14-ounce can tomatoes, chopped
14-ounce can red kidney beans
1 small red bell pepper, roughly chopped
1 medium zucchini, sliced into chunks
Cauliflower flowerets
2 carrots, roughly chopped
$\frac{1}{2}$ Tbsp tomato paste
1 tsp dried, sweet basil
1 tsp oregano
1-1$\frac{1}{2}$ cups broth

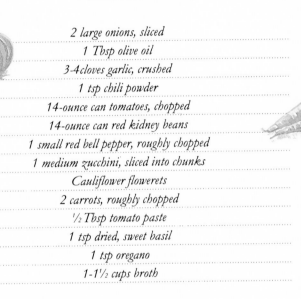

Sauté the onions in the oil until soft. Add the garlic and cook for 1 minute. Add the chili powder and cook for a further minute. Add the rest of the ingredients and simmer for 25-30 minutes. Serve on a bed of brown rice.
Time: Preparation takes about 15 minutes, cooking takes 30 minutes.

Savory Rice Cake

An excellent way to use up leftover rice.

SERVES 2-4

1 medium onion, minced
1 clove garlic, crushed
2 Tbsps olive oil
1 Tbsp fresh thyme, chopped
1 red pepper, thinly sliced
1 green pepper, thinly sliced
4 eggs, beaten
Salt and freshly ground black pepper
6 Tbsps cooked brown rice
3 Tbsps plain yogurt
6 Tbsps grated vegetarian Cheddar cheese

Fry the onion and garlic in the olive oil until soft. Add the thyme and pepper and fry gently for 4-5 minutes. Beat the eggs with the salt and pepper. Add the cooked rice to the thyme and pepper, followed by the eggs. Cook over a moderate heat, stirring from time to time until the eggs are cooked underneath.

Spoon the yogurt on top of the partly-set egg and sprinkle the cheese over the top. Place under a broiler and broil under modern heat until puffed and golden. Serve immediately.
Time: Preparation takes about 15 minutes, cooking takes 15 minutes.
Serving Idea: Garnish with fresh thyme and serve with a green salad.

Zucchini & Pine Nut — Lasagne —

This unusual lasagne will leave your guests curious as to the delicious combination of ingredients.

SERVES 4

12 strips of whole-wheat lasagne
6 Tbsps pine nuts
2 Tbsps butter
1½ pounds zucchini, trimmed and sliced
1¼ cups ricotta cheese
½ tsp grated nutmeg
1 Tbsp olive oil
1 large eggplant, sliced
⅔ cup water
2 tsps shoyu sauce (Japanese soy sauce)
6 Tbsps grated Cheddar cheese

Place the lasagne in a large roasting pan and completely cover with boiling water. Leave for 10 minutes and then drain. Place the pine nuts in a dry skillet and toast gently for 2 minutes. Set aside. Melt the butter and cook the zucchini with a little water until just tender. Combine the zucchini, pine nuts, and ricotta cheese. Add the nutmeg and mix together thoroughly.

In a separate pan, heat the olive oil and sauté the eggplant for 4 minutes. Add the water and shoyu and simmer, covered, until soft. Liquidize until smooth, adding a little extra water to the blender if necessary. Place 4 strips of lasagne on the bottom of a greased 2-quart rectangular dish and top with half the zucchini mixture. Place 4 more strips of lasagne over the zucchini and add half the eggplant sauce  followed by the rest of the zucchini. Cover with the remaining lasagne and the rest of the sauce. Sprinkle the grated cheese over the top and bake in an oven preheated to 375 degrees, for 40 minutes or until the cheese is golden-brown.

Time: Preparation takes about 30 minutes, cooking takes 50 minutes.

Serving Idea: Serve with a crunchy mixed salad and Creamy Jacket Potatoes – bake the potatoes until soft, remove the potato from the skins, and mash with a little milk, butter, and seasoning. Cool a little and place the mixture in a piping bag with a large nozzle. Pipe the mixture back into the potato shells and re-heat when required. Note: You will need to cook a couple of extra potatoes in order to have plenty for the filling.

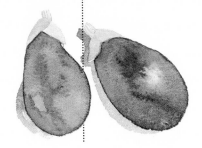

Vegetable Niramish

This highly fragrant curry is ideal to serve as part of a larger Indian meal. Vary the vegetables according to what you have to hand.

SERVES 4

1 small eggplant
Salt
3 Tbsps vegetable oil
1 onion, sliced
1 green chili, seeded and finely chopped
1 tsp cumin seeds
1 large potato, peeled and cut into chunks
½ cup cauliflower flowerets
1 small green pepper, sliced
2 small carrots, peeled and thickly sliced
1 tsp each ground coriander, turmeric, and chili powder
⅔ cup vegetable broth
1 tsp chopped fresh coriander (cilantro)
Juice of 1 lime
Chilies to garnish

Cut the eggplant into chunks, sprinkle liberally with salt, and allow to stand for 30 minutes. Rinse well and drain on kitchen paper.

Heat the oil in a saucepan and fry the onion, green chili, and cumin seeds for 2 minutes. Stir in the potato and fry for 3 minutes. Add the eggplant, cauliflower, pepper, and carrots and fry for another 3 minutes. Stir in the spices and fry for 1 minute, then add the broth. Cover and simmer gently for 30 minutes until all the vegetables are tender, adding a little more broth if needed.

Add the coriander and lime juice and simmer for 2 minutes. Serve garnished with chilies.

Time: Preparation takes about 20 minutes, plus standing. Cooking takes about 40 minutes.

Serving Idea: Serve with boiled rice and a simple salad.

Vegetarian Shepherd's Pie

This unusual pie will serve 2 people without any accompaniment and 4 people if served with vegetables.

SERVES 2-4

½ cup brown lentils

¼ cup pot barley

2 cups broth or water

1 tsp broth granules

1 large carrot, diced

½ onion, minced

1 clove garlic, crushed

4 Tbsps walnuts, roughly chopped

1 tsp vegetarian gravy powder or thickener

Salt and freshly ground black pepper

1 pound potatoes, cooked and mashed

Simmer the lentils and barley in 1¼ cups of broth with the stock granules for 30 minutes. Meanwhile, cook the carrot, onion, garlic, and walnuts in the remaining broth for 15 minutes or until tender. Mix the gravy powder or thickener with a little water, add to the carrot mixture, and stir over a low heat until thickened.

Combine the lentils and barley with the carrot mixture; season and place in an ovenproof dish. Cover with the mashed potato and bake in an oven preheated to 350 degrees for about 30 minutes, until browned on top.

Time: Preparation takes 15 minutes, cooking takes 1 hour.

Serving Idea: Garnish with broiled tomatoes and serve with vegetables in season, such as broccoli, collard greens, etc.

Oven Baked Spaghetti

A convenient way to cook this favorite mid-week meal.

SERVES 4

8 ounces whole-wheat spaghetti, cooked

2 x 14-ounce cans tomatoes, roughly chopped

1 large onion, grated

1 tsp oregano

Salt and freshly ground black pepper

8 thin slices vegetarian Cheddar cheese

2 Tbsps grated vegetarian Parmesan cheese

Grease four individual ovenproof dishes and place a quarter of the spaghetti in each one. Pour the tomatoes over the top. Add the onion, sprinkle with oregano and season well. Arrange the cheese slices over the top of the spaghetti mixture.

Sprinkle with Parmesan and bake in an oven preheated to 350 degrees, for 30 minutes.

Time: Preparation takes 10 minutes, cooking takes 20-25 minutes.

Serving Idea: Serve with garlic bread.

Watchpoint: When cooking spaghetti, remember to add a few drops of oil to the boiling water to stop it sticking together.

Cook's Tip: Oven-baked Spaghetti may be cooked in one large casserole if required, but add 10 minutes to the cooking time.

Tri-Colored Tagliatelle & Vegetables

A delicious Italian dish that is ideal for an informal supper party.

SERVES 4

8 ounces tri-colored tagliatelle (mixture of tomato, spinach, and egg pasta)

4 Tbsps butter or margarine

1 large onion, sliced

1 cup broccoli flowerets

2 red peppers, sliced

2 cloves garlic, crushed

2 tsps chopped fresh rosemary

6 Tbsps finely grated vegetarian Cheddar cheese

Salt and freshly ground black pepper

Cook the pasta in plenty of lightly salted, boiling water for 10 minutes, or as directed on the packet. Meanwhile, melt half the butter or margarine in a skillet, add the onion, and sauté for 4 minutes. Add the broccoli and peppers and continue to cook for 5 minutes or until all the vegetables are tender.

Place the garlic, rosemary, and remaining fat in a separate saucepan and heat gently for a few minutes until the fat melts and the flavors combine. When the pasta is cooked, drain well and return to the pan. Strain the garlic mixture through a sieve over the pasta – this gives a very subtle hint of garlic and rosemary to the pasta. Add the cooked vegetables and cheese. Season to taste and toss well before serving.

Time: Preparation takes about 10 minutes, cooking takes about 15 minutes.

Nut & Herb Bulgar

Bulgar wheat is cooked similarly to rice, although it requires soaking, and can be used as an alternative to many rice dishes.

SERVES 4

1 Tbsp walnut oil

1 Tbsp vegetable oil

1 red pepper, cut into short sticks

1 onion, chopped

2 Tbsps pine nuts

1 small cucumber, diced

1 Tbsp chopped fresh coriander (cilantro)

1 Tbsp chopped fresh mint

2 Tbsps chopped fresh parsley

1 cup bulgar wheat

2 cups vegetable broth

Mint sprigs, to garnish

Heat the oils in a large saucepan and fry the pepper, onion, and pine nuts for 5 minutes. Add the cucumber, herbs, and bulgar wheat, then pour in the broth. Bring gently to a boil, stir, cover, and simmer gently for 10-15 minutes or until the broth has been absorbed, stirring occasionally. Serve hot or cold, garnished with sprigs of mint.

Time: Preparation takes about 10 minutes, cooking takes about 20 minutes.

Serving Idea: Serve with a mixed salad.

Variation: Use brown rice instead of bulgar wheat in this recipe and increase the cooking time accordingly.

Ratatouille Pie with Cheese & — Peanut Pastry —

A colorful dish to make in the fall when eggplant and zucchini are inexpensive and plentiful.

SERVES 4-6

Ratatouille
2 Tbsps olive oil

2 onions, chopped

4 tomatoes, sliced

1 eggplant, sliced

3 zucchini, finely sliced

2 sticks celery chopped

White sauce
4 Tbsps all-purpose flour

4 Tbsps butter or margarine

2 cups milk

Pastry
4 Tbsps butter

1 cup self-rising flour

4 Tbsps finely grated vegetarian cheese

4 Tbsps salted peanuts, finely chopped

A little milk

Beaten egg to glaze

Put the oil and all the vegetables into a large pan and cook gently for about 20 minutes or until soft. To make the sauce, melt the margarine in a separate pan, stir in the flour, and cook for 2 minutes, stirring constantly. Gradually add the milk and bring to boiling point. Stir the sauce into the vegetable mixture and put into an ovenproof dish.

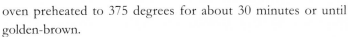

Rub the butter into the flour, and add the cheese and peanuts.
Add a little milk and roll out the pastry. Place on top of the ratatouille mixture, trim, and brush with beaten egg. Bake in an oven preheated to 375 degrees for about 30 minutes or until golden-brown.

Time: Preparation takes 30 minutes, cooking takes 1 hour.

Serving Idea: Serve with bundles of julienne vegetables – carrots, jicama, turnips etc.

Variation: Sliced green pepper can be used in place of the celery.

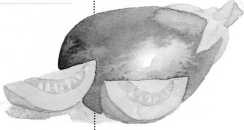

Zucchini & Sweetcorn Savory

This is an excellent way to use up leftover pasta.

SERVES 4

1 Tbsp oil

1 medium onion, chopped

4 zucchini, sliced

7-ounce can corn kernels, drained

¾ cup cooked pasta shapes

Large pinch of dried oregano

1 Tbsp tomato paste

Salt and freshly ground black pepper

Sauce

2 Tbsps butter or margarine

2 Tbsps whole-wheat flour

1 ¼ cups skim milk

3 Tbsps white wine

4 Tbsps grated sharp vegetarian cheese

Topping

2 Tbsps whole-wheat bread crumbs

2 tsps sunflower seeds

Heat the oil in a skillet and sauté the chopped onion until soft. Add the sliced zucchini and brown lightly. Mix in the sweetcorn, cooked pasta, oregano, and tomato paste, and stir. Season lightly and transfer the mixture to an oiled ovenproof dish.

Make the cheese sauce by melting the margarine and stirring in the flour to make a roux. Heat gently for a few minutes and then add the milk and wine, stirring all the time, to make a smooth sauce. Add the grated cheese and stir until it melts into the sauce. Remove from the heat and pour it over the vegetable mixture. Top with the bread crumbs and sunflower seeds. Bake in an oven preheated to 350 degrees, for about 20 minutes, until the dish is brown and bubbling.

Time: Preparation takes about 30 minutes, cooking takes 20 minutes.

Serving Idea: Serve with broiled tomatoes and creamed potatoes.

Conchiglie with
—Two Sauces—

A very low fat pasta dish with two delicious sauces.

SERVES 4

1 pound cooked conchiglie (pasta shells)

Tomato sauce

1 large onion, minced

1 tsp broth granules

3 Tbsps water

1 clove garlic, crushed

¹/₂ tsp dried thyme

Pinch of ground rosemary

14-ounce can tomatoes

Mushroom sauce

1 cup oyster mushrooms

2 Tbsps butter or margarine

1 tsp broth granules

4 Tbsps thick-set plain yogurt

Minced fresh parsley for garnish

To make the tomato sauce, place the onion, broth granules, water, and garlic in a pan and cook very gently for 7-10 minutes, until the onion is soft. Add the thyme and rosemary and cook for 1 minute. Chop the tomatoes and add to the pan together with the tomato juice. Bring to a boil and boil rapidly, until the sauce has reduced and thickened.

To make the mushroom sauce, chop the mushrooms finely. Melt the margarine in a pan and add the broth granules and mushrooms. Simmer very gently for 10-15 minutes. Remove from the heat and stir in the yogurt. Heat gently until hot, but do not allow to boil.

Divide the pasta between 4 serving dishes. Pour the tomato sauce over one half of the pasta and the mushroom sauce over the other half. Sprinkle the minced parsley between the two sauces. Serve at once.

Time: Preparation takes about 20 minutes, cooking, including the pasta, takes 35 minutes.

Cook's Tip: The sauces may be prepared in advance, refrigerated, and reheated when required. Use fresh or dried pasta, but remember that dried pasta takes longer to cook.

Variation: Both sauces are suitable for use on their own – just double the quantities given.

Sweet Bean Curry

This excellent curry will freeze well for up to six weeks.

SERVES 4

¾ cup red kidney beans, soaked overnight

2 Tbsps butter or margarine

1 onion, sliced

1 apple, cored and chopped

¾ cup mushrooms, sliced

1 Tbsp curry powder

2 Tbsps all-purpose flour

2½ cups bean broth or bean broth and water

Salt to taste

1 Tbsp lemon juice

1 Tbsp chutney

4 Tbsps yellow raisins

¼ cup creamed coconut, grated or chopped

Drain the beans, put into a large pan, and cover with cold water. Bring to a boil and boil vigorously for 10-15 minutes; reduce the heat and boil for about an hour, until the beans are tender but still whole.

Melt the butter or margarine and cook the onion until it is very brown. Add the apple and mushrooms and cook for 2-3 minutes. Add the curry powder and flour and cook for 2 minutes, stirring all the time. Gradually add the bean broth and stir until smooth. Add the seasoning, lemon juice, chutney, yellow raisins, and beans and cook for 10-15 minutes. Just before serving, add the creamed coconut, and stir until dissolved.
Time: Preparation takes 25 minutes. Cooking time, including the beans, 1 hour 25 minutes.

Piper's Pie

Accompany this attractive dish with carrots and corn kernels for the perfect family meal.

SERVES 4

1 pound potaotes, peeled and diced

¾ cup mung beans

4 leeks

1 onion, sliced

½ tsp dillweed

1 inch fresh ginger root, chopped or finely grated

1 Tbsp concentrated apple juice

1 tsp miso

Boil the potatoes and mash with a little butter and seasoning. In a separate pan, cover the mung beans with water and boil for 15-20 minutes until soft.

Meanwhile, generously butter an ovenproof casserole dish and put in the leeks, onion, dill, ginger and concentrated apple juice. Mix well. Drain the beans, reserving the broth, and add to the casserole dish. Dissolve the miso in a little of the bean broth and mix into the casserole which should be moist but not too wet. Cover and cook in an oven preheated to 400 degrees for 30-45 minutes, stirring a couple of times during the cooking and adding a little more bean broth if necessary.

Remove from the oven and cover with a layer of mashed potatoes. Brown the top in the oven or under the broiler.
Time: Preparation takes 20 minutes, cooking takes 50-60 minutes.
Variation: A small can of corn kernels may be added to the pie before covering with the mashed potatoes.

Stuffed Summer Squash

A great way of using large summer squashes.

SERVES 4

1 medium summer squash
6 Tbsps fresh brown bread crumbs
2-4 Tbsps milk
4 eggs, hard cooked
$\frac{1}{2}$ cup grated cheese
Salt and pepper
Pinch of freshly grated nutmeg
1 egg, beaten
A little margarine or butter
Parsley and 1 sweet red pepper for garnish

Wash the squash well, cut in half lengthwise, and scoop out the seeds. Place in a well-greased roasting pan or ovenproof dish. Soak the bread crumbs in the milk. Chop the hard-cooked eggs and add to the bread crumbs, together with the cheese, seasoning, and nutmeg. Bind the mixture with the beaten egg. Pile into the marrow halves and dot with small pieces of margarine or butter. Pour a little water around the squash and bake in an oven preheated to 375 degrees for 35-40 minutes, until the squash is tender and the top is nicely browned. (If the top is browning too quickly, cover with aluminum foil.) Serve on a large dish garnished with parsley and red pepper rings.
Time: Preparation takes 25 minutes, cooking takes 35-40 minutes.
Serving Idea: For a Thanksgiving dinner, use pumpkin instead of squash, garnish with cranberries, and surround with sliced red or yellow bell peppers, chopped lettuce, and watercress.

Express Vegetable Pie

Any cooked, leftover vegetables may be used for this quick and easy pie.

SERVES 4

1 large onion, minced
2 Tbsps margarine
2 sticks celery, diced
6 Tbsps cashew nuts, chopped and dry-roasted
1$\frac{1}{2}$ pounds mixed frozen vegetables (peas, corn, carrot, turnip, diced peppers, jicama, etc.)
2 tsps tomato paste
$\frac{2}{3}$ cup water or broth
$\frac{1}{2}$-1 tsp broth granules
Salt and freshly ground black pepper
3-4 large potatoes
About 1 tsp butter
A little milk

Sauté the onion in the margarine together with the celery and a little water until just tender. Add the remaining ingredients apart from the potatoes, butter and milk. Simmer for 3-5 minutes, adding a little more water if the mixture seems too dry. Keep hot.

Cook the potatoes until soft; mash with a tablespoon of butter and a little milk, adding salt and pepper to taste. Turn the vegetable mixture into a casserole dish and cover completely with the mashed potato. Fork over the top roughly, dot with butter, and broil for 3-5 minutes, until golden brown. Serve immediately.
Time: Preparation takes 20 minutes, cooking takes 15 minutes.
Serving Idea: Serve with salad, mushrooms, and pumpkin seeds.

Pasta Spirals with Walnuts & Stilton

This classic combination of walnuts and blue cheese creates an unusual but delicious Italian-style meal.

SERVES 4

1 pound pasta spirals
1¼ cups heavy cream
1 pound vegetarian blue cheese
½ cup walnut halves
Salt and freshly ground black pepper
4 sprigs fresh thyme, to garnish
2 ripe figs, to garnish

Cook the pasta in plenty of lightly salted, boiling water for 10 minutes or as directed on the package. Pour the cream into a saucepan and bring to a boil. Boil rapidly for 3 minutes, then crumble in the blue cheese and stir until it melts. Stir in the walnut halves and season with pepper.

When the pasta is cooked, drain well, rinse with boiling water, and return to the pan. Pour the cream and cheese sauce over the pasta and toss well. Garnish with sprigs of thyme and ½ a ripe fig per plate before serving.

Time: Preparation takes about 5 minutes, cooking takes about 20 minutes.

Cook's Tip: The walnut sauce, or either of the variations, make a superb dipping sauce into which can be dipped crusty bread or fresh vegetables.

Cheese Sandwich Soufflé

Unlike a true soufflé, there is no need to rush this dish to the table as it will not sink. It is equally delicious served hot or cold.

SERVES 4

1 Tbsp wholegrain mustard
8 slices whole-wheat bread
2 tomatoes, sliced
¾ cup grated vegetarian Cheddar cheese
2 eggs, beaten
2½ cups milk
1 tsp dried basil
Salt and freshly ground black pepper
Parsley sprigs, to garnish

Preheat the oven to 350 degrees. Spread equal amounts of mustard over four slices of the bread. Arrange the tomato slices over the mustard-spread bread, and sprinkle with the grated cheese. Use the remaining four slices of bread to cover the cheese. Place the cheese-and-tomato sandwiches in a large, shallow dish or 4 smaller individual dishes into which they will just fit. Beat together the eggs, milk, and basil, and season well. Pour this over the bread, and leave to stand for 30 minutes to allow the bread to soak up the milk mixture.

Bake for 40-45 minutes or until the milk mixture is set. Serve garnished with sprigs of parsley.

Time: Preparation takes about 10 minutes, plus 30 minutes standing time. Cooking takes about 45 minutes.

Vegetarian Paella

This tasty dish is perfect served with crusty bread and a green salad.

SERVES 4-6

4 Tbsps olive oil
1 large onion, chopped
2 cloves garlic, crushed
1/2 tsp paprika
1 1/2 cups long-grain brown rice
3 3/4 cups broth
3/4 cup dry white wine
14-ounce can chopped tomatoes
1 Tbsp tomato paste
1/2 tsp tarragon
1 tsp basil
1 tsp oregano
1 red pepper, roughly chopped
1 green pepper, roughly chopped
3 sticks celery, finely chopped
2 cups mushrooms, washed and sliced
1/4 cup snow peas, trimmed and halved
1/2 cup frozen garden peas
4 Tbsps cashew nut pieces
Salt and freshly ground black pepper

Heat the oil and fry the onion and garlic until soft. Add the paprika and rice, and continue to cook for 4-5 minutes, until the rice is transparent. Stir occasionally. Add the broth, wine, tomatoes, tomato paste, and herbs and simmer for 10-15 minutes.

Add the pepper, celery, mushrooms, and snow peas and continue to cook for another 30 minutes, until the rice is ready. Add the peas, cashew nuts, and seasoning to taste. Heat through and place on a large heated serving dish. Sprinkle the parsley over the top and garnish with lemon wedges and olives.

Time: Preparation takes 20 minutes, cooking takes 45 minutes.

Cook's Tip: To prepare in advance, undercook slightly, add a little more broth or water, and reheat. Do not add the peas until just before serving otherwise they will lose their color.

Corn & Parsnip Flan

Serve this quiche with jacket potatoes filled with cottage cheese and chives. Substitute jicama for the parsnips.

SERVES 6

Base

⅓ cup soft margarine

1½ cups whole-wheat flour

1 tsp baking powder

Pinch of salt

4-6 Tbsps ice-water

1 Tbsp oil

Filling

1 large onion, minced

1 clove garlic, crushed

2 Tbsps butter or margarine

2 large parsnips, steamed and roughly mashed

¾ cup corn kernels, frozen or canned

1 tsp dried basil

Salt and freshly ground black pepper

3 eggs

⅔ cup milk

6 Tbsps grated vegetarian Cheddar cheese

1 medium tomato, sliced

Rub the margarine into the flour, baking powder, and salt until the mixture resembles fine bread crumbs. Add the water and oil and work together lightly. The mixture should be fairly moist. Leave for half an hour. Roll out the dough and use it to line a 10-inch pie pan. Prick the dough and bake blind at 425 degrees for about 8 minutes.

Meanwhile, sauté the onion and garlic in the butter or margarine until soft and golden. Add the parsnips, sweetcorn, and basil and season to taste. Beat the eggs and add the milk. Add to the vegetable mixture and stir over a low heat until the mixture just begins to set.

Pour into the quiche base and top with the grated cheese and sliced tomato. Bake at 375 degrees for 15-20 minutes or until the cheese is golden-brown.

Time: Preparation takes about 40 minutes, cooking takes 30 minutes.

Cook's Tip: The partial cooking of the whole mixture before placing in the pastry base helps to keep pastry from becoming soggy and considerably reduces the cooking time.

Vegetable Stew with Herb — Dumplings —

The ideal meal to warm up a cold winter's night

SERVES 4-6

1 large onion

2 pounds mixed vegetables (carrot, rutabaga, parsnip, turnip, cauliflower, etc.)

2½ cups vegetable broth

Salt and freshly ground black pepper

Flour or gravy powder to thicken

Dumplings

1 cup whole-wheat self-rising flour

4 Tbsps vegetarian shortening

1 tsp mixed herbs

¼ tsp salt

Chop the onion into large pieces. Peel and prepare the vegetables and chop into bite-sized pieces. Put the onion and vegetables into a pan and cover with the broth. Bring to a boil and simmer for 20 minutes. Season to taste.

Mix a little flour or gravy powder with a little water and stir into the stew to thicken. Place the ingredients for the dumplings in a bowl and add just enough water to bind. Shape the mixture into 8 small dumplings. Bring the stew to a boil and drop in the dumplings. Cover and allow to simmer for 10 minutes. Serve at once.

Time: Preparation takes 10 minutes, cooking takes 30 minutes
Serving Idea: Serve with boiled potatoes.
Variation: The mixed herbs may be omitted when making the dumplings or minced fresh parsley and a squeeze of lemon juice may be used instead.

Savory Bean Pot

Serve this exciting mixture with rice or jacket potatoes and a salad.

SERVES 4

2 Tbsps vegetable oil

2 vegetable broth cubes, crumbled

2 medium onions, chopped

2 dessert apples, peeled and grated

2 medium carrots, grated

3 Tbsps tomato paste

1¼ cups water

2 Tbsps white wine vinegar

1 Tbsp mustard powder

1 tsp dried oregano

1 tsp ground cumin

2 tsps brown sugar

Salt and freshly ground black pepper

1 pound cooked red kidney beans

About 2 Tbsps sour cream

Heat the oil in a nonstick skillet. Add the crumbled broth cubes, onions, apples, and carrots. Sauté for 5 minutes, stirring continuously. Mix the tomato paste with the water and add together with all the other ingredients, apart from the beans and cream. Stir well, cover and simmer for 2 minutes. Add the beans and tip the mixture into an ovenproof casserole. Cover and cook in an oven preheated to 350 degrees, for 35-40 minutes. Add a little more water after 20 minutes if necessary. Top with swirls of sour cream and serve.

Time: Preparation takes 20 minutes, cooking takes 45 minutes.

Fifteen Minute Goulash

This quick and easy goulash is best served with baked potatoes.

SERVES 4

1 onion, minced
1 clove garlic, crushed
2 carrots, diced
3 medium zucchini, diced
2 Tbsps olive oil
1 Tbsp paprika
Pinch of nutmeg
1 heaped Tbsp freshly chopped parsley
1 Tbsp tomato paste
14-ounce can tomatoes
1 cup cooked or 14-ounce can red kidney beans, drained
²/₃ cup tomato juice or broth
Salt and freshly ground black pepper
Sour cream or yogurt to serve

Put the onion, garlic, carrots, and zucchini into a pan with the olive oil and sauté for 5 minutes, until softened. Stir in the paprika, nutmeg, parsley, and tomato paste. Add the rest of the ingredients, except cream or yogurt, and cook over a low heat for 10 minutes.

Pour onto a heated serving dish and top with a little sour cream or yogurt.

Time: Preparation takes 10 minutes, cooking takes 15 minutes.

Variation: Vary the type of bean used – try pink beans, pinto beans or chickpeas.

Mushroom Stroganoff

A great favorite that is much appreciated by all age groups.

SERVES 4

2 medium onions, sliced
5 sticks celery, chopped
4 Tbsps butter or margarine
1 pound button mushrooms
¹/₂ tsp mixed herbs
¹/₂ tsp basil
1 large heaping Tbsp all-purpose flour
1¹/₄ cups vegetable broth
Salt and freshly ground black pepper
¹/₃ cup sour cream or yogurt
Chopped fresh parsley

Put the onions and celery into a large pan together with the butter or margarine and sauté over a low heat until the onions are transparent. Add the mushrooms and cook for 2-3 minutes, until the juices run. Add the mixed herbs and basil. Stir in the flour and cook for 1 minute. Add the broth and seasonings and allow to cook gently for 8-10 minutes.

Remove from the heat, stir in the sour cream, and adjust the seasoning if necessary. Heat very gently to serving temperature but do not allow to boil. Garnish with the chopped parsley and serve at once.

Time: Preparation takes 10 minutes, cooking takes 20 minutes.

Serving Idea: Serve on a bed of Walnut Rice – cook enough rice to serve 4-6 people and carefully fold in seasoning, a little butter, 1 crushed clove of garlic, and 4 Tbsps finely chopped walnuts.

Cheese & Tomato Pasta

This favorite Italian dish is perfect served as a lunch or supper dish and will be popular with all the family.

8 ounces tagliatelle verdi
1 Tbsp vegetable oil
1 onion, chopped
1 cup thinly sliced mushrooms
1 Tbsp tomato paste
14-ounce can chopped tomatoes
2 Tbsps dried mixed herbs
1½ cups grated vegetarian Cheddar cheese
Salt and freshly ground black pepper

Cook the pasta in plenty of lightly salted, boiling water for 10 minutes or as directed on the package. Meanwhile, heat the oil in a skillet and sauté the onion until beginning to soften. Add the mushrooms and fry for 3 minutes. Stir in the tomato paste, tomatoes, and herbs, and simmer gently while the pasta cooks.

When the pasta is cooked, stir most of the cheese into the sauce. Season. Drain the pasta and pile it onto a serving dish. Spoon the sauce into the center and top with the remaining cheese.
Time: Preparation takes about 10 minutes, cooking takes about 20 minutes.
Serving Idea: Serve with a mixed Italian salad and hot garlic bread.
Variation: Use any variety of pasta shapes in this recipe.
Cook's Tip: Fresh pasta is readily available and very quick to cook. You will need about twice the weight of dried pasta.

Savory Grain Casserole

Serve as a complete meal for 2 people or serve accompanied with lightly steamed vegetables for 4 people.

⅓ cup brown rice
⅓ cup split peas
2 sticks celery, very finely chopped
1 medium onion, minced
1 cup chopped mushrooms
14-ounce can tomatoes, drained and chopped or
1 cup tomatoes, skinned and chopped
½ tsp dill seeds
½ tsp thyme
2 Tbsps shoyu sauce (Japanese soy sauce)
1 egg, beaten
½ cup vegetarian Cheddar cheese, grated

Cover the rice with water and cook for 10-15 minutes, then drain. Cover the split peas with water and cook for 20 minutes until just tender but not mushy, then drain. Meanwhile, combine the celery, onion, mushrooms, tomatoes, dill, thyme, shoyu, and the egg in a large bowl. Stir in the rice and peas. Place the mixture in a greased, ovenproof casserole dish and bake in an oven preheated to 350 degrees, for 45 minutes. Remove from the oven and sprinkle with the grated cheese. Return to the oven for 10 minutes until the cheese has melted. Serve at once.
Time: Preparation takes 10 minutes, cooking takes 1 hour 45 minutes.

Cabbage Parcels

The nutty texture and flavor of these filled cabbage leaves is ideally complemented by the mushroom-and-tomato sauce.

½ cup soup pasta
8-12 large cabbage leaves, washed
1 hard-cooked egg, finely chopped
4 Tbsps walnuts, chopped
1 Tbsp chopped fresh chives
2 Tbsps fresh minced parsley
1 tsp fresh minced marjoram
Salt and freshly ground black pepper
1¼ cups vegetable broth
1 Tbsp walnut oil
1 onion, minced
1 green pepper, chopped
14-ounce can chopped tomatoes
1 cup chopped button mushrooms
2 Tbsps tomato paste
1 bay leaf
Pinch of sugar

Cook the pasta in plenty of lightly salted, boiling water for 8 minutes or as directed on the package. Remove the thick stems from the base of the cabbage leaves and then blanch the leaves in boiling water for 3 minutes. Drain, and refresh in cold water.

When the pasta is cooked, drain it well and mix with the egg, walnuts, and herbs, and season. Divide the pasta mixture between the cabbage leaves, fold up to enclose the filling completely, and secure with tooth picks. Place in a shallow, ovenproof casserole dish and add the broth. Cover and bake in an oven preheated to 350 degrees for 40 minutes.

Heat the oil in a skillet and fry the onion and pepper for 5 minutes, or until soft. Stir in the remaining ingredients, season, and cook gently for 10 minutes. Remove the cabbage parcels from the casserole dish with a slotted spoon, and serve with the sauce poured over them.

Time: Preparation takes about 30 minutes, cooking takes about 1 hour.

Vegetable Couscous

Couscous is a popular dish in North Africa, where it is often cooked by steaming over an accompanying stew.

SERVES 4

2 Tbsps vegetable oil

2 onions, sliced

3 cloves garlic, crushed

1 large potato, peeled and diced

4 carrots, peeled and sliced

2 small turnips, peeled and diced

1 green pepper, diced

1 tsp each, ground cumin, coriander (cilantro), turmeric, and chili powder

14-ounce can chickpeas, drained

2¹/₂ cups vegetable broth

8 zucchini, trimmed and sliced

4 Tbsps yellow raisins

2 Tbsps ready-to-eat dried apricots, chopped

Salt and freshly ground black pepper

1 pound couscous

2 Tbsps plain yogurt (optional)

Heat the oil in a large saucepan and fry the onions until beginning to soften. Add the garlic, potato, carrots, turnip,s and green pepper and sauté for 5 minutes. Stir in the spices and cook for 1 minute. Add the chickpeas, broth, zucchini, raisins, and apricots. Season with salt and pepper. Bring gently to a boil and simmer for 30 minutes.

Meanwhile, place the couscous in a large bowl and cover with boiling water. Allow to stand for 15 minutes, then place in a steamer lined with cheesecloth and steam for 15 minutes. Pile the couscous onto a serving platter and serve the vegetables on top. Garnish with a little yogurt if wished.

Time: Preparation takes about 20 minutes, cooking takes about 40 minutes.

Preparation: The couscous can be placed in a steamer and steamed on top of the vegetables if wished.

Lentil Savory

This dish is quick and easy to prepare and very nutritious.

SERVES 4

¾ cup lentils
½ tsp basil
½ tsp mixed herbs
2 medium onions, chopped
4 Tbsps butter or margarine
2 Tbsps tomato paste
14-ounce can tomatoes
1 tsp brown sugar
Salt and freshly ground black pepper
6 slices vegetarian Cheddar cheese
⅔ cup sour cream

Soak the lentils overnight. Add the lentils to a saucepan with their soaking liquid. Add the herbs and simmer until tender. Sauté the onion in the fat until soft. Add the lentils and the other ingredients, apart from cheese and cream. Simmer for 15 minutes, until thickened, and pour into a greased ovenproof dish. Cover with the cheese and cream and broil, or bake in an oven preheated to 350 degrees, until the cheese has melted.

Time: Preparation takes 15 minutes, cooking takes 35-45 minutes.

Cook's Tip: The sour cream can be served separately if desired.

Serving Idea: Serve hot with a mixed salad.

Freezing: This lentil savory will freeze well but do not cover it with cream and cheese until you reheat it.

Chestnut Hot-Pot

This enticing hot-pot is perfect served with a lightly cooked green vegetable.

SERVES 4-6

1½ pounds potatoes
3 medium onions
1 cup brown lentils
1 cup chestnuts
Salt and freshly ground black pepper
2 tsps broth granules
2 cups warm water
4 Tbsps butter or margarine

Peel and slice the potatoes and onions thinly. Put layers of potatoes, onions, lentils, and chestnuts into a greased pie pan, ending with a layer of potatoes. Season well between each layer. Dissolve the granules in the warm water and pour this over.

Dot with margarine and cover. Bake in an oven, preheated to 350 degrees, for an hour or until the potatoes are tender. Increase the heat to 400 degrees, remove the lid from the casserole, and return to the oven for 10-15 minutes, until the potatoes are crispy and golden-brown.

Time: Preparation takes 20 minutes, cooking takes 1 hour 15 minutes.

Variation: Dried chestnuts may be used but need to be soaked overnight in broth or water.

Nutty Spaghetti

An easy-to-make lunch or supper dish.

SERVES 4

8 ounces spaghetti
3 cups boiling, salted water
1 onion, minced
2 Tbsps sunflower oil
2½ tsps curry powder
¾ cup tomato juice
3 Tbsps crunchy peanut butter
1 Tbsp lemon juice
Lemon twists and peanuts for garnish

Boil the spaghetti until just tender and drain well. Fry the onion in the oil until golden-brown. Stir in the curry powder, tomato juice, peanut butter, and lemon juice. Simmer for 5 minutes and then stir into the spaghetti.

Time: Preparation takes about 10 minutes, cooking takes 25 minutes.

Serving Idea: Serve garnished with lemon twists and peanuts.

Variation: Almond butter and blanched almonds can be used in place of the peanut butter and peanuts.

Spicy Black-Eyed Peas

A delicious dish from the West Indies.

SERVES 4

1 cup black-eyed peas, soaked and cooked
4 Tbsps vegetable oil
1 large onion, minced
2 cloves garlic, crushed
1 tsp ground cinnamon
½ tsp ground cumin
Salt and freshly ground black pepper
⅔ cup bean broth or water
2 Tbsps tomato paste
1 Tbsp shoyu sauce (Japanese soy sauce)
2 large tomatoes, skinned and chopped
1 Tbsp chopped parsley

Drain the beans well and retain the cooking liquid. Heat the oil and fry the onion and garlic for 4-5 minutes until soft. Stir in the cinnamon, cumin, and seasoning and cook for a further 2 minutes. Add the beans, bean broth, tomato paste, shoyu sauce, and tomatoes. Stir and bring to a boil. Simmer for 15-20 minutes, until thick. Check the seasoning. Serve sprinkled with chopped parsley.

Time: Preparation takes 20 minutes. Cooking time, including the beans, 1 hour 35 minutes.

Serving Idea: Serve over cooked pasta or rice.

Variation: Turtle beans can be used in place of black-eyed peas.

Indian Vegetable Curry

A wonderfully tasty curry which has the added advantage of freezing well.

SERVES 4

Spices

2 tsps turmeric

1 tsp cumin seeds

1 tsp mustard seed

1 tsp fenugreek

4 tsps coriander (cilantro) seeds

½ tsp chili powder

1 tsp chopped fresh root ginger

1 tsp black peppercorns

1 pound onions, minced

Clarified butter or vegetable oil

1¼ cups sterilized milk

2 Tbsps white wine vinegar

14-ounce can tomatoes, blended with their juice.

1 Tbsp tomato paste

2 tsps brown sugar

1 tsp vegetable broth concentrate dissolved in a little boiling water

4 cups chopped mushrooms or mixed vegetables

(e.g. mushrooms, cauliflower, carrots, potatoes, okra)

Grind the spices together – this should make 3 Tbsps of curry powder. Fry the onions in the clarified butter or vegetable oil until golden. Add the spices, reduce the heat, and cook for 3 minutes, stirring constantly. Add the milk and vinegar and stir well. Add the liquidized tomatoes, tomato paste, sugar and broth.

Bring to a boil, cover, and simmer very gently for 1 hour. Add the vegetables and cook until tender – about 30 minutes.

Time: Preparation takes 30 minutes, cooking takes 1 hour 30 minutes.

Serving Idea: Serve with boiled brown rice, chappatis (Indian breads) and Cucumber Raita. To make Cucumber Raita, combine diced cucumber with yogurt, a little chopped mint, a pinch of chili powder, cumin, and seasoning to taste.

Freezing: The curry sauce will freeze well for up to 3 months; so it is well worth while making double the quantity.

Chana Masala

An excellent dish to serve hot as an entrée or cold as an accompaniment to a nut loaf.

SERVES 4

1 large onion, chopped
4 cloves garlic, crushed
¼ inch fresh root ginger, peeled and minced
3 Tbsps clarified butter
1 Tbsp ground coriander
2 tsps cumin seed
¼ tsp cayenne pepper
1 tsp turmeric
2 tsps roasted cumin seed, ground
1 Tbsp amchur (dried mango powder) or 1 Tbsp lemon juice
2 tsps paprika
14-ounce can tomatoes
3 cups cooked chickpeas (1½ cups uncooked)
1 tsp garam masala or curry powder
½ tsp salt
1 fresh green chili, finely chopped

Sauté the onion, garlic, and ginger in the clarified butter until soft. Add all the spices and fry over a low heat for 1-2 minutes stirring constantly. Add the tomatoes, roughly chopped, together with their juice. Add the cooked chickpeas. Cook for 30 minutes over a medium heat. Add the garam masala, salt, and chili. Stir well and serve.

Time: Preparation takes about 15 minutes, cooking takes 30 minutes.

Chickpea Patties

These patties are nice cold and are useful for a packed lunch or picnic.

SERVES 4

1 pound cooked chickpeas or 2 14-ounce cans chickpeas
1 onion, minced
2 cloves garlic, crushed
2 medium potatoes, cooked and mashed
2 Tbsps shoyu sauce (Japanese soy sauce)
2 tsps lemon juice
Freshly ground black pepper
Whole-wheat flour
Oil for frying

Put the chickpeas into a large bowl and mash well. Add the onion, garlic, potato, shoyu, lemon juice, and pepper. Mix together well. With floured hands, shape heaped tablespoonfuls of the mixture into small patties. Coat each patty with flour and refrigerate for 1 hour. Heat a little oil and gently fry the patties on each side until golden-brown.

Time: Preparation takes 15 minutes, cooking takes about 15 minutes.

Serving Idea: Serve with a hot, spicy tomato sauce.

Freezing: Cook and freeze for up to 2 months.

Asparagus and Olive Quiche

An interesting combination which gives a new twist
to a classic dish.

MAKES 2 x 10-inch QUICHES

2 x 10-inch part-baked pastry cases
6 eggs
2½ cups light cream
1 tsp salt
Pinch of nutmeg
Salt and freshly ground black pepper
2 Tbsps flour
2 cans green asparagus tips
¾ cup pitted green olives
2 onions, minced and sautéed in a little butter until soft
6 Tbsps grated vegetarian Cheddar cheese
2 Tbsps vegetarian Parmesan cheese
4 Tbsps butter

Whisk the eggs with the cream. Add the salt, nutmeg, and seasoning. Mix a little of the mixture with the flour until smooth, then add to the cream mixture. Arrange the asparagus tips, olives, and onion in the pastry shells and pour the cream mixture over the top. Sprinkle with the grated Cheddar and Parmesan. Dot with the butter and bake in an oven preheated to 375 degrees, for 25 minutes. Reduce the heat to 350 degrees for a further 15 minutes, until the quiches are golden.
Time: Preparation takes 20 minutes, cooking takes 40 minutes.

Sweet Potato & Bean Pasties

These pasties are a tasty addition to any lunch-box or
picnic basket.

SERVES 4

8 ounces whole-wheat pie dough
½ medium onion, minced
1 clove garlic, crushed
1 Tbsp oil
½ tsp grated fresh root ginger
¼-½ tsp chili powder
¼ tsp ground turmeric
½ tsp ground cumin
1 tsp ground coriander
¼ tsp mustard powder
1 medium sweet potato, cooked and finely diced
1 cup green beans, chopped into ½-inch lengths
2 tbsps water or broth
Salt and freshly ground black pepper

Fry the onion and garlic in the oil until soft. Add the ginger and all the spices and stir. Add the diced potato, beans, and water or broth and cook gently for 4-5 minutes or until the beans begin to soften. Allow the mixture to cool, then season well. Roll out the dough into 4 circles. Place a quarter of the filling in the center of each circle and dampen the edges of the pastry with a little water. Join the pastry together over the filling. Make a small hole in each pasty and glaze with milk or egg. Bake in an oven preheated to 400 degrees, for 10-15 minutes.
Time: Preparation, including making the pastry, takes 25 minutes. Cooking takes 15-20 minutes.

Beany Lasagne

This tasty lasagne is suitable for a family meal or entertaining friends.

SERVES 4-6

8 strips whole-wheat lasagne
1 large onion, minced
1 Tbsp vegetable oil
1-2 cloves garlic, crushed
1 cup cooked adzuki beans
1 green pepper, chopped
14-ounce can chopped tomatoes
1 Tbsp tomato paste
1 tsp dried basil
1 tsp dried oregano
Shoyu sauce (Japanese soy sauce) or salt
Freshly ground black pepper

Sauce
2 tbsps butter or margarine
2 tbsps whole-wheat flour
2 cups milk or soya milk
4 tbsps grated vegetarian Cheddar cheese (optional)
Salt and freshly ground black pepper

Cook the lasagne in a large pan of boiling, salted water for 8-10 minutes until *al dente*. Drain well and drape over a cooling rack or the sides of a colander to cool and prevent sticking together. Soften the onion in a little oil, sprinkling with a little salt to draw out the juice. Add the crushed garlic, beans, green pepper, chopped tomatoes, tomato purée, and herbs.

Simmer for about 10 minutes or until the vegetables are tender. Add the shoyu sauce and season to taste.

To make the sauce, combine the margarine, flour, and cold milk. Gradually bring to a boil, stirring continuously. When thickened, allow to simmer, partly covered, for approximately 6 minutes. Stir the cheese into the sauce and season. Layer the lasagne in a greased dish in the following order: half the bean mix, half the pasta, rest of the bean mix, rest of the pasta. Top with the cheese sauce.

Bake in an oven preheated to 350 degrees for 35 minutes or until golden-brown and bubbling. Serve in the dish in which it has been cooked.

Time: Preparation takes 20 minutes, cooking takes about 60 minutes.

Serving Idea: Serve with a green salad.

Cook's Tip: Pre-cooked lasagne can be used, but it is important to add an extra amount of liquid to the dish so that the pasta has enough to absorb while cooking.

Bulgar Risotto

This makes a quick lunch dish and is particularly handy if unexpected guests call.

SERVES 3-4

¹/₂ cup bulgar wheat
1 medium onion, minced
2 sticks celery, finely chopped
1-2 cloves garlic, crushed
1 Tbsp butter
1 small red pepper, diced
1 small green pepper, diced
¹/₂ tsp dried mixed herbs
4 Tbsps peanuts, chopped
1 soup cube dissolved in ¹/₂ cup boiling water
2 tsps shoyu sauce (Japanese soy sauce)
¹/₃ cup corn kernels
¹/₃ cup peas
Salt and freshly ground black pepper
Juice of ¹/₂ a lemon

Put the bulgar wheat into a bowl and cover with boiling water. Leave for about 10 minutes, after which time the water will have been absorbed and the wheat swollen. Meanwhile, place the onion, celery, and garlic into a saucepan and sauté for a few minutes in the butter. Add the peppers, herbs, nuts, and soup cube. Simmer over a low heat for about 8 minutes.

Add the bulgar wheat, shoyu, corn, peas, and seasoning, and mix together well. Continue cooking for a further 5 minutes.

Mix in the lemon juice and transfer to a heated serving dish. Serve immediately.

Time: Preparation takes 15 minutes, cooking takes 20 minutes.

Serving Idea: Serve with a crisp green salad.

Watchpoint: If the risotto is too dry, add a little more water or broth.

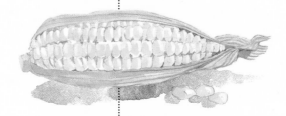

Deep Mushroom Pie

A delicious pie and so adaptable. Serve with salad or potatoes, and a green vegetable.

SERVES 4

Filling

1 Tbsp vegetable oil

3 cups mushrooms, cleaned and chopped

1 cup mixed nuts, finely ground

2 medium onions, finely chopped

1 cup wholewheat bread crumbs

2 eggs, beaten

1 tsp dried or 2 tsps fresh chopped thyme

1 tsp dried or 2 tsps fresh chopped marjoram

1 Tbsps shoyu (Japanese soy sauce)

Salt and freshly ground black pepper to taste

Small quantity of broth to achieve right consistency if necessary

Whole-wheat dough

3 cups whole-wheat flour

Pinch of salt

1 tsp baking powder

½ cup vegetable shortening

½ cup water plus extra boiling water as necessary

Beaten egg to glaze

Heat the oil in a large saucepan and gently fry the onion until soft. Add the finely chopped mushrooms and cook until the juices begin to run. Remove from the heat and add all the other filling ingredients to give a thick but not dry consistency, adding a little broth or water if necessary. Allow to cool.

To prepare the dough, first sift the flour, salt, and baking powder into a large mixing bowl. Cut the fat into small pieces and melt in a saucepan. Add the cold water and bring to a fierce, bubbling boil. Immediately pour this into the center of the flour and mix vigorously with a wooden spoon until glossy. When the mixture is cool enough to handle, knead it into a ball. Divide the mixture into two-thirds and one-third, placing the one-third portion in an oiled plastic bag to prevent drying out. Use the two-thirds portion to line the base and sides of a 7-inch springform pan, pressing it down and molding it into shape. Spoon in the mushroom filling and press down firmly, mounding it in the center. Roll out the remaining dough to just larger than the pan and place on top of the pie, pinching the edges together to seal.

Trim off any excess dough and glaze generously with beaten egg. Cut or prick vents in the lid to allow the steam to escape. Bake in an oven preheated to 425 degrees, for 20 minutes. Reduce to 375 degrees and bake for a further hour.

Unmold and serve on an attractive platter surrounded by watercress and twists of lemon and cucumber.

Time: Preparation takes about 35 minutes, cooking takes 1 hour 20 minutes.

Stuffed Eggplant

When filled with this delicious stuffing, these interesting vegetables make a substantial hot meal.

SERVES 2

2 large eggplant

2 Tbsps vegetable oil

1 onion, chopped

1 clove garlic, crushed

1 green pepper, chopped

½ cup mushrooms, chopped

14-ounce can chopped tomatoes

1 Tbsp tomato paste

2 tsps chopped fresh basil

Pinch of sugar

Salt and freshly ground black pepper

2 Tbsps whole-wheat bread crumbs

½ tsp dried oregano

2 Tbsps walnuts, chopped and lightly toasted

4 Tbsps grated vegetarian Cheddar cheese (optional)

Salad garnish, to serve

Cut the eggplant in half and score the flesh in a criss-cross pattern with a sharp knife. Sprinkle liberally with salt and set aside for 30 minutes. Rinse the eggplant and scoop out the flesh, leaving a border to form a firm shell. Blanch the eggplant shells in boiling water for 3 minutes, then drain. Chop the flesh.

Heat the oil in a skillet and sauté the onion and garlic until softened. Stir in the pepper, mushrooms, and eggplant flesh and fry for 5 minutes. Add the tomatoes, tomato paste, basil, and sugar. Season well. Place the hollowed-out eggplant shells in a lightly greased, shallow ovenproof dish and pile the tomato mixture into the shells. Mix together the bread crumbs, oregano, walnuts, and cheese, if using. Sprinkle this over the eggplants. Bake in an oven preheated to 375 degrees, for 20 minutes. Serve with a salad garnish.

Time: Preparation takes about 20 minutes, plus standing. Cooking takes about 40 minutes.

Sesame Stir-Fry

This recipe can be prepared in advance and cooked quickly for a convenient oriental-style meal.

SERVES 4

2 Tbsps vegetable oil

½ tsp grated fresh root ginger

1 Tbsp sesame seeds

4 Tbsps snow peas

1 stick celery, sliced

2 baby corn cobs, cut in half lengthwise

4 Tbsps water chestnuts, thinly sliced

2 Tbsps thinly sliced mushrooms

2 green onions (scallions), sliced diagonally

½ red pepper, sliced

¼ head (Napa) cabbage, leaves washed and shredded

½ cup beansprouts

1 Tbsp cornstarch

2 Tbsps soy sauce

1 Tbsp sherry

½ tsp sesame oil

4 Tbsps water

Heat the oil in a wok or large skillet and fry the ginger and sesame seeds for 1 minute. Add the snow peas, celery, baby corn, water chestnuts, mushrooms, green onions (scallions) and pepper. Stir-fry for 5 minutes or until the vegetables are beginning to soften slightly. Add the cabbage and beansprouts and toss over the heat for 1-2 minutes.

Combine the remaining ingredients in a small bowl, then add to the pan. Continue cooking until sauce thickens slightly and serve immediately.

Time: Preparation takes about 15 minutes, cooking takes about 10 minutes.

Variation: Use bite-size pieces of jicama if water chestnuts are not available.

Kidney Bean Curry

Kidney beans are wonderfully enhanced by the flavor of the spices in this delicious curry.

SERVES 4

2 Tbsps vegetable oil

1 large onion, sliced

2 cloves garlic, crushed

2 green chilies, seeded and chopped

2 tsps grated fresh root ginger

1 tsp chili powder

1 tsp ground coriander

1 tsp ground cumin

1 tsp garam masala

1 cinnamon stick

14-ounce can chopped tomatoes

1 bay leaf

2 cups canned red kidney beans (drained)

Salt and freshly ground black pepper

Chopped fresh coriander (cilantro), to garnish

Heat the oil in a large saucepan and fry the onion, garlic, and fresh chilies for 5 minutes. Stir in the spices and cook for 1 minute. Add the tomatoes, bay leaf, and kidney beans. Season to taste. Cover, and simmer gently for 30 minutes or until the flavors are well blended. Remove the cinnamon stick and bay leaf. Garnish with chopped coriander (cilantro).

Time: Preparation takes about 20 minutes, cooking takes about 35 minutes.

Serving Idea: Serve with a cucumber raita or hot lime pickle and long-grain rice. Indian breads, if available, are also excellent accompaniments.

Preparation: Great care must be taken when preparing fresh chilies. Wear rubber gloves to prevent the juice being left on the fingers and getting into your eyes or mouth. If this should happen, rinse with plenty of cold water.

Festive Roast

Never again will Thanksgiving or Christmas dinner be a problem with this festive roast.

SERVES 8

2 Tbsps sunflower oil

2 medium onions, minced

2 cloves garlic, crushed

1 pound cashew nuts, finely ground

2 cups whole-wheat bread crumbs

2 beaten eggs or 4 Tbsps soya flour mixed with a little water

1 heaped tsp mixed herbs

2 tsps yeast extract or 1 soup cube

1¼ cups boiling water

Salt and pepper

Heat the oil and fry the onion and garlic until soft. Place the onions and garlic in a large bowl. Add all the other ingredients and mix well. Butter or line a 2-pound loaf pan and spoon in the mixture. Cover with a double thickness of foil and cook in an oven preheated to 350 degrees, for about 1 hour 20 minutes, until firm. Allow to cool for about 10 minutes in the pan before unmolding.

Time: Preparation takes about 15 minutes, cooking takes about 1 hour 20 minutes.

Freezing: An excellent dish to freeze, cooked or uncooked, although a slightly better result is obtained if frozen uncooked and thawed overnight in the refrigerator.

Serving Idea: Serve with a wine sauce or gravy and decorate with berry sprigs or holly.

Carrot and Cashew Nut Roast

A delicious roast to serve hot, although the full flavor of the caraway seeds and lemon is more prominent when the roast is served cold.

SERVES 6

1 medium-sized onion, chopped

1-2 cloves garlic, crushed

1 Tbsp olive or sunflower oil

2 cups cooked, mashed carrots

2 cups ground cashew nuts

1 cup whole-wheat bread crumbs

1 Tbsp light tahini

1½ tsps caraway seeds

1 tsp yeast extract or 1 soup cube

Juice of ½ a lemon

⅓ cup cooking liquid from the carrots, or water

Salt and freshly ground black pepper

Fry the onion and garlic in the oil until soft. Mix together with all the other ingredients and season to taste. Place the mixture in a greased 2-pound loaf pan. Cover with foil and bake in an oven preheated to 350 degrees, for 1 hour.

Remove the foil and bake for a further 10 minutes. Leave to stand in the pan for at least 10 minutes before unmolding.

Time: Preparation takes 20 minutes, cooking takes 1 hour 10 minutes.

Serving Idea: Serve hot with roast potatoes and a green vegetable, or cold with a mixed green salad.

Side Dishes

Side dishes can transform a rather ordinary entrée into a memorable meal. If for convenience you have prepared a simple vegetable patty, broiled dish, or omelet, then go to town with an unusual accompaniment. Because vegetarians eat more vegetables than meat-eaters by incorporating them more often into entrées, there's more reason than ever to take the trouble to serve accompanying vegetables in a rather more elaborate way.

It's also nice to give seasonal produce a distinctive touch when it is at its most plentiful such as in Brussels Sprouts with Hazelnuts (p. 90) or Spinach with Blue Cheese and Walnuts (p. 88).

Other accompaniments are perfect at any time of the year – don't forget rice as a simple, nutritious side-dish. Rice is a grain which contains useful protein so it is helpful in boosting the protein content of vegetarian foods, and is especially beneficial when served with a nut- or bean-based dish.

Plain old potatoes shouldn't be overlooked either; if the oven is being used for a slow-cooking dish, add a baked potato in to cook too. Baby new potatoes can be served with just about any dish, garnished with a little mint, chives, or parsley from the herb garden. Other root vegetables work well too, often in association with each other. Instead of just plain mashed potatoes or hash browns, try adding grated carrot, jicama, turnip or celeriac (celery root).

The microwave oven should not be neglected for cooking vegetables. Small quantities of fresh vegetables can be microwaved in just the minimum of water and this is the ideal way to cook frozen vegetables straight from the freezer. Always remember to time food carefully as it is all too easy to overcook vegetables in the microwave oven, and to lose that *al dente* texture.

Whether microwaving vegetables or cooking them by conventional means, always try to remember the golden rules of vegetable (and fruit) preparation. To ensure maximum retention of vitamin C, prepare them immediately before cooking, in the minimum of water, to limit the loss of the water-soluble vitamins B and C. Cook until just tender – overcooking destroys the texture, flavor, and vitamin C content, as does keeping vegetables warm in a heated dish until required. Always save the cooking liquid from vegetables and use it in sauces, soups, and gravies.

Finally, don't forget how easy it is to stir-fry vegetables to liven up a main course. Finely sliced root vegetables, shredded green leaves, sliced peppers, mushrooms or zucchini and broccoli all make colorful stir-fries. Cook quickly in a wok or large skillet in a little oil, with a hint of garlic, ginger, or soy sauce to give an Oriental touch to your vegetables.

Spinach with Blue Cheese — & Walnuts —

This hot salad is an ideal accompaniment to a rich meal.

SERVES 4

4 cups spinach leaves, washed
2 Tbsps butter or margarine
Pinch of grated nutmeg
Salt and freshly ground black pepper
½ cup walnuts, roughly chopped
½ cup vegetarian blue cheese, crumbled

Remove any tough leaves from the spinach and place the leaves in a saucepan with just the water left clinging to them after washing. Cook over a low heat for 5-10 minutes, until the spinach wilts. Put the spinach on a plate and press a second plate firmly on top to remove the excess water.

Melt the butter or margarine in the pan and stir in the spinach, along with the nutmeg and seasoning. Stir well to coat evenly. Quickly stir in the walnuts and cheese, tossing the ingredients together lightly. Serve quickly before the cheese melts too much.

Time: Preparation takes about 15 minutes, cooking takes about 10 minutes.

Serving Idea: Serve with nut roasts, vegetable cutlets, or pâtés.

Variation: Use diced tofu instead of cheese in this recipe for a vegan alternative.

Braised Fennel

The aromatic, aniseed flavor of fennel makes it an ideal accompaniment to rich casseroles and vegetable bakes.

SERVES 4

2 large fennel bulbs
2 tsps chopped fresh lovage
½ cup vegetable broth
2 Tbsps sherry
½ tsp celery seeds or celery seasoning

With a sharp knife, cut away the thick root end of the fennel bulbs. Trim away the upper stalks and reserve a little of the green top for garnish. Thickly slice the fennel, separating the strips from each other as you cut. Place the fennel, lovage, broth, and sherry in a saucepan and bring to a boil. Reduce the heat and simmer gently for about 15 minutes, or until the fennel is tender. Drain, and transfer to a warm serving dish. Sprinkle with celery seeds or seasoning and garnish with fennel tops.

Time: Preparation takes about 10 minutes, cooking takes about 15 minutes.

Cook's Tip: If lovage is unavailable, chop some of the leafy fennel tops and use them instead.

Variation: Add 1 peeled, cored and thinly sliced tart apple to the fennel for a delicious variation.

Wild Rice Pilau

Although expensive, a little wild rice goes a long way when mixed with long-grain rice, adding a special flavor and texture to the dish.

SERVES 4

¾ cup long-grain rice

¼ cup wild rice

2 Tbsps vegetable oil

1 piece cassia bark or ½ stick cinnamon

4 black or green cardamom pods, lightly crushed

8 cloves

4 black peppercorns

1 piece star anise

2½ cups vegetable broth

4 Tbsps dry white wine

4 Tbsps flaked almonds

4 Tbsps raisins

Place the long-grain rice and wild rice in two separate sieves and rinse thoroughly under running water, draining well. Heat half the oil in a saucepan and fry the spices for 1 minute. Add the wild rice and cook for 1 minute, stirring constantly. Add the broth and wine, and bring to a boil. Stir, cover, and simmer for 25 minutes.

Heat the remaining oil in a skillet, add the long-grain rice, and cook, stirring, for 1 minute. 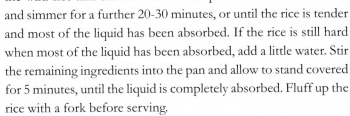 Add some of the hot liquid from the wild rice to the skillet and stir in. Pour the long-grain rice and liquid into the wild rice and stir well. Cover the pan and simmer for a further 20-30 minutes, or until the rice is tender and most of the liquid has been absorbed. If the rice is still hard when most of the liquid has been absorbed, add a little water. Stir the remaining ingredients into the pan and allow to stand covered for 5 minutes, until the liquid is completely absorbed. Fluff up the rice with a fork before serving.

Time: Preparation takes about 5 minutes, cooking takes about 1 hour.

Serving Idea: Serve with vegetarian curries, casseroles, or chili.

Variation: Add some cooked chopped mixed vegetables instead of the nuts and raisins.

Carrot & Parsnip Medley

The perfect accompaniment to the recipe for Festive Roast (see page 85).

SERVES 8

⅓ cup butter or margarine
8 medium carrots, peeled and sliced
4 parsnips, peeled and cut into rings
1 tsp ground ginger
½ tsp grated nutmeg
Salt and freshly ground black pepper
Juice of 1 lemon
2 tsps superfine sugar
Chopped fresh parsley

Melt the butter or margarine in a large pan and add the carrots and parsnips. Sauté very gently for 2-3 minutes then add the ginger, nutmeg, seasoning, lemon juice, and enough water to cover the vegetables. Cover and simmer for 15-20 minutes until the vegetables are soft and the liquid has evaporated.

Add the sugar and increase the heat, tossing the vegetables until they are glossy. Transfer to a heated serving dish and sprinkle with the chopped parsley.

Time: Preparation takes 10 minutes, cooking takes 20-25 minutes.
Variation: If you cannot get parsnips, use turnips or rutabaga.
Cook's Tip: Lemons yield more juice if you first roll them backwards and forwards on a kitchen work surface with your hands, using medium pressure.

Brussels Sprouts with — Hazelnuts —

This is a delicious variation on Brussels sprouts with chestnuts and will soon become a firm favorite.

SERVES 4

1 pound Brussels sprouts, trimmed
2 Tbsps butter or margarine
4 Tbsps hazelnuts
Salt and freshly ground black pepper

Cut a cross in the stalks of any large sprouts and cook in lightly salted boiling water for 10-15 minutes or until tender. Just before the sprouts are cooked, melt the butter or margarine in a skillet and fry the hazelnuts, stirring frequently, until browned.

When the sprouts are cooked, drain well and return to the pan. Add the hazelnuts and toss well. Transfer to a serving dish and serve with a good sprinkling of black pepper.

Time: Preparation takes about 10 minutes, cooking takes about 15 minutes.
Serving Idea: Serve with broiled dishes and nut roasts.
Variation: Use almonds, Brazil nuts, or pecans instead of hazelnuts in this recipe.

Pommes Noisettes

These delicious cheesy potato balls will complement any meal, whether a sophisticated dinner party or an intimate family lunch.

SERVES 4-6

1 pound potatoes, peeled and cut into chunks
2 Tbsps butter or margarine
Salt and freshly ground black pepper
4 Tbsps finely grated vegetarian Colby or Jack cheese
4 Tbsps ground hazelnuts
Oil for shallow-frying
Fresh parsley or watercress sprigs, to garnish

Cook the potatoes until tender; mash them well. Add the butter or margarine, seasoning, and cheese, and fork through until well combined. Refrigerate until completely cold. Shape spoonfuls of the mashed potatoes into 1-inch balls.

Spread the nuts on a plate and roll the potato balls in the nuts, making sure they are well coated. Heat the oil in a skillet and fry the potato until golden, turning frquently. Serve garnished with parsley or watercress.

Time: Preparation takes about 15 minutes, plus chilling. Cooking takes about 30 minutes.

Serving Idea: Serve with broiled dishes, salads or roasts.

Preparation: The noisettes can be prepared up to 24 hours in advance.

Perfect Potatoes

Potatoes become extra special when teamed up with the flavor of onion.

SERVES 5

2 pounds potatoes
1 large onion
Salt and freshly ground black pepper
1¼ cups milk
3 Tbsps butter or margarine

Peel and finely slice the potatoes and onion. Layer the potato slices and onion in a shallow, ovenproof dish, sprinkling each layer with some salt and pepper. Add the milk and dot with the butter or margarine. Bake uncovered in an oven preheated to 350 degrees, for 1-1½ hours or until the potatoes are soft, and golden-brown on top.

Time: Preparation takes 15 minutes, cooking takes 1-1½ hours.

Serving Idea: Serve with broiled mushrooms and tomatoes for a supper dish, or serve with nut roasts or pies.

Freezing: Cool quickly, cover with foil, and place in a freezer bag. Defrost at room temperature for 4-6 hours and reheat at 375 degrees for about 30 minutes.

Variation: Place a layer of finely sliced tart apples in the bottom of the dish.

Sri Lankan Rice

Serve this rice hot as an accompaniment to vegetable curries or lentil dishes.

SERVES 12

3 Tbsps sunflower oil

1 medium onion, minced

2 cloves garlic, crushed

2 tsps ground cumin

2 tsps ground coriander (cilantro)

1 heaping tsp paprika

2 tsps turmeric

$\frac{1}{4}$ tsp chili pepper or cayenne pepper

$\frac{2}{3}$ cup Basmati rice, washed and drained

$1\frac{1}{2}$ cups milk

1 tsp salt

Freshly ground black pepper to taste

1 cup snow peas, topped, tailed and cut in half

1 cup mushrooms, washed and sliced

$\frac{2}{3}$ cup canned corn kernels, drained

4 Tbsps yellow raisins, washed and soaked

Heat the oil in a large nonstick skillet. Gently fry the onion and garlic for 4-5 minutes. Add the cumin, coriander, paprika, turmeric, and chili, and fry for a further 3-4 minutes – do not allow the mixture to burn. Add the washed rice, mix well with the onions and spices, and cook for about 2 minutes. Add the milk, salt, and pepper. Stir gently, bring to a boil, cover, and simmer until all the liquid is absorbed and the rice is cooked – approximately 15-20 minutes.

While the rice is cooking, steam the snow peas, mushrooms, corn, and raisins and fold into the rice. Cool and unmold onto a serving platter.

Time: Preparation takes 15 minutes, cooking takes 25-30 minutes.

Serving Idea: Sprinkle with 2 Tbsps of freshly chopped coriander (cilantro) or parsley.

Variation: Other lightly steamed vegetables may be used according to season and personal taste – broccoli flowerets, diced carrots, peas, and sliced green bell peppers.

Leeks Provençale

This classic method of serving vegetables is exceptionally well suited to leeks as the flavors combine so well.

SERVES 4

6 leeks, washed and trimmed

1 Tbsp olive oil

2 cloves garlic, crushed

4 tomatoes, skinned, seeded, and chopped

1 tsp dried thyme

2 Tbsps chopped fresh parsley

4 Tbsps dry white wine

Salt and freshly ground black pepper

Sprigs of fresh parsley, to garnish

Cut the leeks into 2-inch pieces. Cook the leeks for 10-15 minutes in lightly salted boiling water, until tender. Heat the oil in a small saucepan and fry the garlic until softened but not colored. Stir in the tomatoes, herbs, and wine and simmer gently for 10 minutes or until the tomatoes are softened. Season to taste. When the leeks are cooked, drain well and place on a serving dish. Spoon the tomato mixture into the dish and turn the leeks in the sauce to coat. Serve garnished with a sprig of parsley.
Time: Preparation takes about 10 minutes, cooking takes about 25 minutes.
Serving Idea: Serve with a nut roast for a filling entrée.

Sweet & Sour Cabbage —with Apple—

This tasty side dish adds a splash of color as well as a lively flavor to any meal.

SERVES 4

3-pound head red cabbage

1 onion, chopped

1 tart apple, peeled, cored, and chopped

4 Tbsps light brown sugar

¼ tsp ground mixed spice

Salt and freshly ground black pepper

1¼ cups vegetable broth

2 Tbsps red wine vinegar

1 Tbsp walnut oil

1 dessert apple, cored and chopped

2 tsps minced fresh parsley

Quarter, core, and shred the cabbage. Layer it in a large saucepan with the onion and tart apple. Sprinkle with the sugar and mixed spice. Season with salt and pepper. Add the broth and vinegar and stir to mix the ingredients well. Cover and cook gently for 45 minutes, stirring occasionally.

Just before the end of the cooking time, heat the oil in a skillet and sauté the dessert apple for 2-3 minutes, until just soft. Remove from the heat and stir in the parsley. Transfer the cabbage to a serving dish and garnish with the apple and parsley.
Time: Preparation takes about 20 minutes, cooking takes about 45 minutes.

Broccoli and Cauliflower Mold

Although this dish takes a little while to prepare, it makes a spectacular addition to the dinner table.

SERVES 4-6

2 cups small broccoli flowerets
1 small cauliflower
3 Tbsps walnut oil
1 Tbsp white wine vinegar
1 tsp mustard powder
½ clove garlic, crushed
Salt and freshly ground black pepper
1 Tbsp olive oil
1 green chili, seeded and minced
5 tomatoes, skinned, seeded, and chopped
1 green bell pepper, finely chopped
1 tsp ground cumin
4 green onions (scallions), minced
Tomato quarters, to garnish

Bring a saucepan of water to a boil, add the cauliflower, and cook for 5 minutes. Add the broccoli, cook a further 10 minutes, then drain well.

Combine the walnut oil, vinegar, mustard, garlic, salt, and pepper in a small bowl and whisk with a fork. Pour the dressing over the warm vegetables and toss to coat well, taking care not to break them up. Carefully arrange the cauliflower and broccoli in a deep-sided 1-quart bowl, alternating the 2 vegetables and pressing them together lightly to push them firmly into the bowl shape. Cover with a plate and weigh down slightly. Leave to cool, before refrigerating. It is ready for serving as soon as chilled.

Heat the olive oil in a small skillet and fry the chili for 2-3 minutes. Add the tomatoes, pepper, cumin, and green onions (scallions). Cook for 5 minutes. Season with salt and pepper, allow to cool, then refrigerate well before serving. To serve, carefully unmold the cauliflower onto a serving plate, and spoon the tomato salsa around the base. Garnish with tomato quarters.

Time: Preparation takes about 20 minutes, plus chilling. Cooking takes about 20 minutes.

Zucchini Rolls

These artistic little vegetable rolls are an impressive accompaniment to a sophisticated meal.

SERVES 4

2 carrots, peeled and cut into thin sticks
2 green peppers, cut into strips
4 green onions (scallions), trimmed
Salt and freshly ground black pepper
1 tsp chopped fresh basil or thyme
2 large zucchini
Juice of 1 lemon
Bunch of fresh chives
2 Tbsps butter or margarine
2 Tbsps vegetable oil

Cook the carrots and green peppers for 5 minutes in boiling water until just softened. Drain well and place in a mixing bowl. Shred the green onions (scallions) lengthwise and add to the carrots and pepper. Season the vegetables, add the chopped herbs, and toss together thoroughly. Trim the zucchini and carefully cut lengthwise into very thin slices. Sprinkle with the lemon juice. Lay out the zucchini strips on the work surface and arrange bundles of the vegetables in piles across them. Carefully roll up the zucchini strips around the vegetables. Secure them by tying at each end with chives.

Melt the butter or margarine with the oil in a skillet and sauté the vegetable bundles for 10 minutes, turning frequently until the zucchini are cooked and the vegetables are hot.
Time: Preparation takes 20 minutes, cooking takes 20 minutes.

Tasty Tomato Sauce

Serve this adaptable sauce over stuffed eggplant, squash, or peppers.

SERVES 4

2 Tbsps pine nuts
Pinch of salt
1 tsp sunflower oil
1 onion, chopped
Pinch of chili powder
3 cloves
14-ounce can tomatoes

Place the pine nuts in a skillet and dry roast them. Remove when they are lightly browned and sprinkle with the salt. Fry the onion in the sunflower oil until soft. Add the chili powder and cloves. Fry for 1 minute. Add the tomatoes, bring to a boil, and simmer for 10 minutes. Cool slightly and remove the cloves. Purée the mixture in a blender and return to pan. Add the pine nuts and reheat gently.
Time: Preparation takes 10 minutes, cooking takes 15 minutes.
Watchpoint: Dry-roast the pine nuts over a low heat, stirring continuously, otherwise they will burn.

Desserts

When it comes to dessert, most people can be tempted by a little serving of something sweet. Choose your final course with care to balance with the rest of the meal. From a nutritional point of view, if a meal has been quite light on protein with the emphasis on fresh vegetables, rather than dairy produce, beans, or nuts, now's the time to serve a dairy-based dessert – a cheescake perhaps, or a heavier, double-crust pie or crumble, or even a deliciously different fruit pizza (see Hot Apple Pizza p.101).

Fruit is full of vitamins and fiber and forms a nutritious basis for many popular desserts, whether hot, cold, or frozen. While it's easy to stock the freezer with storebought ice creams and sorbets, there's nothing quite like a home-made ice to impress your guests. Choose either a rich cream or custard-based ice or a refreshing, tangy fruit sorbet, such as Strawberry Sorbet (p.138). Fruit fools, light and easy on the stomach, make a similarly simple end to a meal, perhaps served with a home-made cookie or piece of shortcake. And why not serve seasonal fruits by serving a Cranberry Whip (p.106) at Thanksgiving?

Giving old family favorites a new twist always works well – Cranberry and Apple Crumble (p.102) for example or Baked Raspberry Apples (p.99). Baked apples are also delicious stuffed with marzipan, a tasty way of boosting the protein level of a dessert. Fruits can be "baked" in the microwave to save time, but watch carefully to avoid overcooking. Cored pears are also suitable for baking, filled with a sweet mixture of fresh or dried fruits and are also delicious topped with home-made creamy topping. Vegans could try a topping of tofu blended with a little sugar and a touch of vanilla or almond flavoring, or even with a hint of spice, such as nutmeg or cinnamon.

One dessert which always proves a winner without piling on the calories is fresh fruit salad. Here the possibilities for combining different fruits are almost endless. Rather than preparing a sugar-based syrup, simply pour over a little fruit juice – orange, freshly pressed apple, grape, or a fruit cocktail blend, with just a hint of fruit liqueur, perhaps. A large bowl full of a myriad different fruits looks stunning, but also consider restricting choice and sticking instead to a color theme. A bowl full of luscious red fruits looks superb, as does a subtle mix of white-fleshed peaches and green from grapes, kiwi fruits, starfruits, and crenshaw or cantaloupe melon. For a different effect again, rather than tossing all the fruits together, try arranging them in different layers. However you serve dessert, choose the ingredients so that you end the meal on a high note.

Windward Fruit Basket

An impressive dessert which is surprisingly easy to prepare.

SERVES 4-6

1 large ripe melon
2 apples
Juice of 1 lime
2 mangoes
2 kiwi fruits
2 cups strawberries, hulled
2 cups raspberries
3 Tbsps honey
2 Tbsps dark rum
4 Tbsps butter

Cut the top off the melon and scoop out the seeds. Using a melon baller, scoop out balls of melon and place in a large bowl. Remove the core from the apples, dice, and toss in the lime juice. Peel and chop the mangoes. Peel and slice the kiwi fruits. Combine the prepared fruits with the whole strawberries and raspberries. Heat the honey, rum, and butter gently until the butter has melted. Cool, and pour over the fruits. Toss gently and fill the melon shell with the fruit mixture. Arrange in sundae glasses and serve immediately.

Time: Preparation takes 20 minutes, cooking takes 2 minutes.

Serving Idea: For a special occasion, make holes around the top of the melon with a skewer and decorate with fresh flowers.

Variation: Use watermelon instead.

Strawberry & Banana Frost

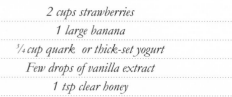

This speedy dessert can be started ahead of time and completed just before serving.

SERVES 4-6

2 cups strawberries
1 large banana
¼ cup quark or thick-set yogurt
Few drops of vanilla extract
1 tsp clear honey

Wash and hull the strawberries and put half of them in the refrigerator. Peel the banana and cut it into pieces. Slice the remaining strawberries in halves, or quarters if they are large, and freeze with the banana until solid. Just before serving, remove the strawberries and banana from the freezer. Place the frozen strawberries and banana with the quark or yogurt, vanilla extract, and honey in a food processor or blender, and process until smooth. You will need to push the mixture down two or three times with a spatula or wooden spoon. Divide the mixture between 4 or 6 individual serving dishes and place the remaining strawberries around the "frosted" mixture. Serve at once.

Time: Preparation takes 10 minutes, freezing takes at least 1 hour.

Variation: Pineapple, raspberries, or apples can be substituted for the above.

Baked Raspberry Apples

A lovely combination which is perfectly complemented
by cream or yogurt.

SERVES 6

2 Tbsps concentrated apple juice
4 Tbsps water
2 Tbsps honey
1 tsp mixed spice
3 very large dessert apples
2 cups raspberries

Put the concentrated apple juice, water, honey, and mixed spice into a large bowl and mix together well. Wash the apples and, with a sharp knife, make deep zig-zag cuts around each apple. Take one half of the apple in each hand and twist gently until the two halves come apart. Remove the core and immerse each apple in the apple juice mixture. Place the apples in an ovenproof dish and bake in an oven preheated to 400 degrees, for 20-25 minutes, until just soft.

Remove from the oven and top with the raspberries. Pour the remaining apple juice mixture over the raspberries. Reduce the oven temperature to 300 degrees and bake for 10 minutes. Serve at once.

Time: Preparation takes 10 minutes, cooking takes 30-35 minutes.
Serving Idea: Serve topped with a spoonful of thick-set yogurt or whipped cream.
Cook's Tip: Frozen raspberries may be used but make sure they are defrosted first.

Raspberry Meringues

Light, pale pink meringues form the basis of this
delightful summer dessert.

SERVES 4

2 egg whites
½ cup superfine sugar
Few drops raspberry flavoring
Few drops of red food coloring (optional)
2 cups raspberries
4 Tbsps raspberry liqueur or sherry
⅔ cup heavy cream, whipped
Cocoa powder, for decoration

Line two cookie sheets with nonstick baking parchment. Whisk the egg whites until stiff, then gradually whisk in the two-thirds of the superfine sugar. Carefully fold in the remaining sugar, flavoring, and a food coloring, if using. Spoon into a piping bag fitted with a plain nozzle and pipe eight heart shapes or rounds.

Place in an oven preheated to 300 degrees for 1½ hours to dry out. Remove from the oven and allow to cool completely. Meanwhile, place the raspberries and liqueur or sherry in a bowl and allow to marinate until required. Whip the cream and use, together with a few of the soaked raspberries, to sandwich the meringues into pairs. Sprinkle the tops with a little cocoa powder and serve any remaining raspberries separately.

Time: Preparation takes about 20 minutes, cooking takes about 1½ hours.
Serving Idea: Serve with extra fruit salad if a more substantial dessert is required.

Peachy Cheesecake

This fairly rich cheesecake has a lovely smooth texture.

SERVES 6

Base
12 graham crackers, crushed into fine crumbs
3 Tbsps melted butter or margarine

Topping
1¼ cups low-fat cream cheese
2 cups sour cream or thickset yogurt
2 Tbsps clear honey
1½ tsps vanilla extract or lemon juice
2 eggs, beaten
1½ Tbsps whole-wheat flour
1 tsp double-acting baking powder
Sliced peaches to decorate

Combine the cracker crumbs, melted butter, and spices and press the mixture in the bottom of a greased 9-inch pie pan or dish. Combine the cream cheese, 1 cup of the sour cream or yogurt, 1 tablespoon honey, ¾ teaspoon vanilla extract, and the eggs. Combine the flour and baking powder and add to the mixture. Pour the mixture onto the cracker base and bake in an oven preheated to 300 degrees for about 20 minutes or until just set. Remove from the oven and increase the temperature to 450 degrees.

Combine the remaining cream or yogurt with the rest of the honey and vanilla extract, and spread over the top of the cake. Smooth over with a knife or spatula. Return to the oven and bake for 5 minutes. Allow to cool before decorating with sliced peaches. Chill thoroughly before serving.

Time: Preparation takes 25 minutes, cooking takes 25 minutes.

Variation: For special occasions decorate with seasonal fruit such as strawberries or raspberries, and chocolate or carob curls.

Cook's Tip: The cake tastes better if refrigerated for 24 hours before eating.

Fruit Salad Cups

These attractive cups of warm fresh fruit make a delightful and unusual ending to a meal.

SERVES 4

2 large oranges
1 small dessert apple
1 slice of fresh pineapple
1 banana
A little orange juice
2 Tbsps caster sugar
1 tsp rum
3 Tbsps shelled, skinned, chopped pistachios
Orange rind, to decorate (optional)

Cut the oranges in half and, using a grapefruit knife, remove the flesh and membranes, leaving just the white parts and rind to form a shell. Set aside. Reserve as much juice as possible and chop the flesh, discarding any tough membranes. Cut the apple into quarters, remove the core, but do not peel. Cut each quarter into bite-size pieces. Remove the skin and any brown "eyes" from the pineapple and cut the flesh into bite-sized wedges. Peel and slice the banana.

Make the reserved juice up to ½ cup with extra orange juice, if necessary. Heat the juice and sugar, and stir until dissolved. Stir in the rum. Mix the prepared fruit into the juice. Just before serving, heat gently to warm the fruit but not cook it. Pile into the orange shells and sprinkle with the chopped pistachios. Decorate with orange zest, if wished, and serve immediately.

Time: Preparation takes 15 minutes, cooking takes 5 minutes.

Hot Apple Pizza

A delicious dessert – perfect with yogurt or cream.

SERVES 4-6

1 Tbsp fresh yeast
4 Tbsps warm water
¼ cup whole-wheat flour
½ cup all-purpose flour
½ tsp ground cinnamon
1 Tbsp butter or margarine
1 Tbsp concentrated apple juice

Topping
2 red-skinned dessert apples
2 Tbsps raisins
2 Tbsps hazelnuts
1 Tbsp concentrated apple juice
1 Tbsp butter or margarine

Cream the yeast with the water, add 1 teaspoon of flour, and leave in a warm place for 10-15 minutes until frothy. Mix together the flours and cinnamon. Rub in the butter. Add the yeast mixture and concentrated apple juice to the flour. Mix to a stiff dough, adding more warm water if necessary. Knead well. Roll the dough into a circle, about 8-9 inches across. Cover with plastic wrap and leave to rise for 10-15 minutes.

Slice the apples evenly and arrange over the base. Sprinkle the raisins, hazelnuts, and concentrated apple juice over the apples and dot with the butter or margarine. Bake in the middle shelf of an oven preheated to 400 degrees, for 15-20 minutes.

Time: Preparation takes, including rising, 45 minutes. Cooking takes 15-20 minutes.

Cranberry and Apple Crumble

Serve hot with plain yogurt or cold with ice cream.

SERVES 4

1½ pounds Rome Beauty or other cooking apples

4 Tbsps superfine sugar

¾ cup fresh cranberries

Crumble

⅓ cup butter or margarine

4 Tbsps shelled sunflower seeds

⅓ cup brown sugar

1¼ cups whole-wheat flour

4 Tbsps jumbo oats

4 Tbsps raw oatmeal

Peel, core, and dice the apples. Place in a saucepan with the sugar and about 2 Tbsps water. Cook gently until just beginning to soften. Add the cranberries and cook for a further minute. Remove from the heat.

Melt the butter or margarine in a small saucepan, add the sunflower seeds, and fry very gently for a few minutes. Mix together the other ingredients in a large bowl, rubbing in the sugar with the fingers if lumpy. Pour the butter and sunflower seeds into this mixture and combine to form a loose crumble.

Place the fruit in a large, shallow ovenproof dish and sprinkle the crumble topping over it. Bake in an oven preheated to 350 degrees, for about 40 minutes or until the top is golden.
Time: Preparation takes about 20 minutes, cooking takes 50 minutes.
Variation: if jumbo oats are not available, use wheat flakes.

Low-Fat Brown Bread Ice Cream

This ice cream is ideal for slimmers.

SERVES 4

3 Tbsps brown bread crumbs

1½ Tbsps brown sugar

3 eggs, separated

1¼ cups thickset lowfat yogurt

2 tsps honey (optional)

Place the bread crumbs on a cookie sheet and cover with the sugar. Place in an oven preheated to 375 degrees for 20 minutes or until they begin to brown and caramelize. Stir once or twice so they brown evenly. Leave aside. Beat the egg whites until stiff.

In a separate bowl, mix the egg yolks into the yogurt and then fold in the egg whites. Add the honey if wished, and fold in evenly. Add the cooled bread crumbs and mix well. Place in the freezer and, when setting point is reached, stir the sides to prevent ice crystals forming. Return to the freezer and leave until set.
Time: Preparation takes 20 minutes, cooking and freezing takes 20 minutes plus 4-5 hours or overnight.
Cook's Tip: Remove from the freezer and place in the refrigerator about ¾ of an hour before serving.
Variation: Maple syrup may be used in place of honey.

St Clement's Sorbet

St. Clement's is possibly the most popular type of water-ice, and it is really quite simple to make at home.

SERVES 6

1¼ cups water

1 cup sugar

4 lemons

1 Tbsp agar (vegetarian gelatin)

2½ cups freshly squeezed orange juice

2 egg whites

Grated orange rind and mint leaves, to decorate

Place the water and sugar in a saucepan, heat gently until the sugar dissolves, bring to a boil, and boil for 5 minutes. Remove from the heat and allow to cool completely. Grate the rind from the lemons with a zester and squeeze the juice. Put a little of the lemon juice in a small bowl and sprinkle with the agar. Dissolve over hot water.

Combine the cooled sugar syrup, lemon rind, juice, dissolved agar, and orange juice; pour into a shallow freezer-proof container and freeze until slushy. Remove from the freezer and beat well to break up the ice crystals. Whisk the egg whites until they stand in soft peaks and beat into the sorbet mixture. Cover and freeze until required. Serve scooped into sundae glasses and decorate with grated orange rind and mint leaves.

Time: Preparation takes about 30 minutes, plus freezing.

Serving Idea: Spoon the sorbet into hollowed out lemon or orange halves.

Fruit Fantasia

A pretty dessert that is simple to prepare and very refreshing.

SERVES 8

1 melon

4 large grapefruit

½ cup black grapes

2 small green dessert apples

2 red dessert apples

⅔ cup light cream

Mint leaves to decorate

Cut the melon into quarters. Remove the flesh, cut into 1-inch pieces and place in a large bowl. Make zig-zag cuts around each grapefruit, halve, remove the flesh, and add to the melon, reserving the grapefruit shells. Halve and seed the grapes. Wash the apples and slice thinly, leaving the skin on. Add to the grapefruit, grapes, and melon. Chill for at least 1 hour. Mix the light cream carefully into the fruit and pile into the grapefruit shells. Decorate with the mint before serving.

Time: Preparation takes about 10 minutes, chilling takes at least 1 hour.

Serving Idea: Serve in individual dishes containing crushed ice and decorated with mint leaves.

Variation: If time is short use seedless grapes and leave them whole.

Crêpes Suzette

Most of the preparation for this spectacular dinner party dish can be done well in advance.

SERVES 4

1 cup all-purpose flour
¼ tsp ground nutmeg
2 eggs
2 tsps vegetable oil
1¼ cups milk
Oil for frying
4 Tbsps butter or margarine
Grated rind of 1 orange
4 Tbsps superfine sugar
1 cup fresh orange juice
2 Tbsps orange-flavored liqueur
2 Tbsps brandy
Orange slices, to decorate

Sift the flour and nutmeg into a mixing bowl and make a well in the center. Drop the eggs, oil, and a little of the milk into the well. Beat with a wooden spoon, slowly incorporating the flour until you have a smooth paste. Gradually beat in the remaining milk, then allow to stand for 20 minutes. Heat a little oil in an 8-inch heavy-based skillet or omelet pan. Pour off any excess oil. Spoon about 3 tablespoons of the mixture into the skillet and tilt so that it coats the base. Cook for about 1 minute, until the underside is golden, then flip or turn over and cook the other side.

Slide the pancake out of the pan and set aside. Repeat until all the mixture has been used, stacking the pancakes on top of each other. Cover them to prevent them drying out.

Melt the butter or margarine in a skillet and stir in the orange rind, sugar, and juice. Cook, stirring, until the sugar dissolves. Add the orange liqueur and allow to boil gently for a few minutes, until the liquid has reduced slightly.

Fold the pancakes into triangles and add to the pan. Cook gently to warm them through. Heat the brandy in a small pan. Set it alight and pour it over the pancakes. Serve when the flames have died down. Decorate with orange slices.

Time: Preparation takes about 35 minutes, plus standing. Cooking takes about 25 minutes.

Freezing: Freeze the pancakes, well wrapped, for up to 6 months. Allow to defrost completely before using.

Halva of Carrots & Cashews

Halva is a traditional Indian dessert made from carrots and cream. Do not let the use of vegetables in a dessert put you off trying this rather special recipe, as the results are really delicious.

SERVES 4-6

2 pounds carrots, peeled

1¼ cups heavy cream

¾ cup dark brown sugar

2 Tbsps clear honey

2 tsps ground coriander (cilantro)

1 tsp ground cinnamon

Pinch of saffron

4 Tbsps butter or margarine

4 Tbsps raisins

½ cup unsalted cashew nuts, chopped

Candied violets, silver sprinkles or grated coconut, to decorate

Grate the carrots using the coarse side of a grater. Place the carrots, cream, sugar, honey, and spices in a large saucepan. Mix well. Cook over a low heat for 15-20 minutes until the carrots are soft, stirring frequently during the cooking to prevent burning.

Add the butter or margarine, raisins, and nuts, stir well, and continue cooking for 10-15 minutes, until the mixture has thickened and the carrots are soft. Cool, then refrigerate untilcold. Pile into serving dishes and decorate with candied violets, silver sprinkles, or coconut.

Time: Preparation takes about 15 minutes, cooking takes about 30 minutes.

Chocolate Orange Cheesecake

Chocolate and orange, a favorite combination for many, are combined in this delicious, rich cheesecake.

SERVES 8-10

6 Tbsps butter or margarine, melted

1 cup chocolate-coated cookies, crushed

1 pound full-fat cream cheese

½ cup superfine sugar

Grated rind and juice of 1 orange

1¼ cups thick-set plain yogurt

1 Tbsp agar (vegetarian gelatin)

3 Tbsps water

4 squares baking chocolate, melted

2 oranges, peeled and segmented

Mix together the butter or margarine and cookies and press into the bottom of an 8-inch springform pan. Chill until firm. Beat together the cream cheese and sugar and then beat in the orange juice and rind. Fold in the yogurt. Sprinkle the agar over the water. Set over hot water until dissolved then stir it into the cream cheese mixture.

Pile the cheese mixture over the cookie base and level the top. Drizzle about two-thirds of the melted chocolate over the top and swirl a skewer through the mixture to create a marbled effect. Chill until set. Transfer to a serving dish and arrange the orange segments on top. Decorate with the remaining chocolate.

Time: Preparation takes about 30 minutes, plus chilling.

Cranberry Whip

A simple and refreshing dessert.

SERVES 4

1 cup fresh cranberries
2 Tbsps clear honey
6 Tbsps whipping cream
½ cup thick-set plain yogurt
Toasted flaked almonds

Rinse the cranberries and simmer in a scant amount of water until softened. Remove from the heat, add the honey, and leave to cool. Whip the cream and gently fold in the yogurt. Combine the yogurt and cream with the cooled cranberries. Divide the mixture between four sundae glasses and decorate with toasted flaked almonds.

Time: Preparation takes 10 minutes, cooking takes 15-20 minutes.

Variation: Dried cranberries may be used at times of the year when fresh are not available.

Apricot Fool

Serve this dessert in individual serving glasses and decorate with curls of chocolate or carob.

SERVES 4

8oz dried apricots
1 ripe banana
1 small carton plain strained yogurt
1 egg
Few squares carob chocolate

Soak the apricots in water for at least 1 hour. Cook until soft then purée. Mash the banana and add to the apricot purée. Fold the yogurt into the fruit mixture. Separate the egg and stir the yolk into fruit mixture. Whisk the egg white until stiff then fold into the fruit mixture.

Time: Preparation takes 10 minutes. Soaking and cooking takes about 2 hours 40 minutes.

Variation: Decorate with toasted almonds.

Plum & Ginger Crisp

Plums and ginger cookies complement each other beautifully in this simple dish.

SERVES 4-6

1 pound dessert plums
4 Tbsps light brown sugar
3 Tbsps orange juice
5 Tbsps unsalted butter or margarine
1 cup crushed ginger cookies
4 Tbsps flaked almonds

Wash and halve the plums and pit them. Place the plums, sugar, and orange juice in a pie pan. Melt the butter or margarine and stir in the crushed cookies and almonds. Mix well to coat all the crumbs. Sprinkle the cookie topping over the fruit and level the top. Bake in an oven, preheated to 350 degrees, for 25 minutes. Cover with foil if the topping begins to brown too much.

Time: Preparation takes about 15 minutes, cooking takes about 25 minutes.

Variation: Use apricots instead of the plums and vanilla wafers or graham crackers flavored with ground cinnamon instead of the ginger cookies.

Strawberry Sorbet

Serve at the end of a very rich meal or between the entrée and dessert, if serving a light summer dinner.

SERVES 4

1 medium lemon
1¼ cups water
¾ cup sugar
1½ pounds strawberries
2 egg whites

Pare the rind from the lemon and put it into the water with the sugar. Heat slowly until the sugar has dissolved, then boil for 5 minutes. Strain and set aside to cool. Hull the strawberries, reserving a few for decoration. Press the remainder through a nylon sieve and add the juice of half the lemon. Whisk the egg whites until very stiff. Combine all the ingredients well. Put into an airtight container and place in the freezer. Remove when half frozen, beat well, and return to the freezer. Place in the refrigerator about 1 hour before serving. Serve in wine glasses and top with the reserved whole berries.

Time: Preparation takes 20 minutes, cooking takes 5 minutes. Freezing takes about 8 hours.

Cook's Tip: It is better to leave the sorbet in the freezer overnight after beating.

Index